WILLIAM LILLY'S

HISTORY

OF HIS

LIFE AND TIMES,

FROM THE YEAR 1602 TO 1681.

Written by Himself,

IN THE SIXTY-SIXTH YEAR OF HIS AGE, TO HIS WORTHY FRIEND,

ELIAS ASHMOLE, ESQ.

PUBLISHED FROM THE ORIGINAL MS.
LONDON, 1715.

LONDON:

RE-PRINTED FOR CHARLES BALDWYN,

NEWGATE STREET.

M.DCCC.XXII.

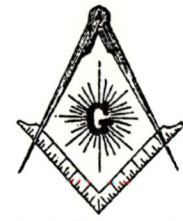

R.Cooper sculp.

WILLIAM LILLY.

From an Original Picture, in the Ashmolean Museum, Oxford.

PUBLISHED BY CHARLES & HENRY BALDWYN, NEWGATE STREET.

ADVERTISEMENT.

PREFIXED TO THE LIVES OF ELIAS ASHMOLE & WILLIAM LILLY.
In 1 vol. 8vo. 1772.

ALTHOUGH we cannot, with justice, compare Elias Ashmole to that excellent Antiquary John Leland, or William Lilly to the learned and indefatigable Thomas Hearne; yet I think we may fairly rank them with such writers as honest Anthony Wood, whose Diary *greatly resembles that of his cotemporary, and intimate friend, Elias Ashmole.*

Some anecdotes, connected with affairs of state; many particulars relating to illustrious

B

persons, and antient and noble families ; several occurrences in which the Public is interested, and other matters of a more private nature, can only be found in works of this kind. History cannot stoop to the meanness of examining the materials of which Memoirs *are generally composed.*

And yet the pleasure and benefit resulting from such books are manifest to every reader.

I hope the admirers of the very laborious Thomas Hearne will pardon me, if I should venture to give it as my opinion, and with much deference to their judgment, that William Lilly's Life and Death of Charles the first *contains more useful matter of instruction, as well as more splendid and striking occurrences, than are to be found in several of those monkish volumes published by that learned Oxonian.*

G.F.Wainwright sculp!

Lilly affords us many curious particulars relating to the life of that unfortunate Prince, which are no where else to be found. In delineating the character of Charles, he seems dispassionate and impartial, and indeed it agrees perfectly with the general portraiture of him, as it is drawn by our most authentic historians.

The History of Lilly's Life and Times *is certainly one of the most entertaining narratives in our language. With respect to the science he professed of calculating nativities, casting figures, the prediction of events, and other appendages of astrology, he would fain make us think that he was a very solemn and serious believer. Indeed, such is the manner of telling his story, that sometimes the reader may possibly be induced to suppose Lilly rather an enthusiast than an impostor. He relates many anecdotes of the pretenders to foretell events, raise spirits, and other impostures, with such seeming candor, and with such an artless simplicity of style, that we are almost persuaded to take his word when he protests such an inviolable respect to truth and sincerity.*

The powerful genius of Shakespeare could carry him triumphantly through subjects the most unpromising, and fables the most improbable: we therefore cannot wonder at the success of such of his plays, where the magic of witches and the incantation of spirits are described, or where the power of fairies is introduced; when such was the credulity of the times respecting these imaginary beings, and when that belief was made a science of, and kept alive by artful and superstitious, knavish, and enthusiastic teachers; what Lilly relates of these people, considered only as matter of fact, is surely very curious.

To conclude; I know no record but this where we can find so just and so entertaining a History of Doctor Dee, Doctor Forman, Booker, Winder, Kelly, Evans, (Lilly's Master,) the famous William Poole, and Captain Bubb Fiske, Sarah Shelborne, and many others.

To these we may add, the uncommon effects of the Crystal, the appearance of Queen Mabb, and other strange and miraculous operations, which owe their origin to folly, curiosity, superstition, bigotry, and imposture.

THE

LIFE

OF

WILLIAM LILLY,

STUDENT IN ASTROLOGY.

Wrote by himself in the 66th Year of his Age, at Hersham, in the Parish of Walton-upon-Thames, in the County of Surry.   *Propria Manu.*

---

* I WAS born in the county of Leicester, in an obscure town, in the north-west borders thereof, called Diseworth, seven miles south of the town of Derby, one mile from Castle-Donnington, a town of great rudeness, wherein it is not remembered that any of

* " William Lilly was a prominent, and, in the opinion of ·many of his cotemporaries, a very important personage in

the farmers thereof did ever educate any of their sons to learning, only my grandfather sent his younger son to Cambridge, whose

the most eventful period of English history. He was a principal actor in the farcical scenes which diversified the bloody tragedy of civil war; and while the King and the Parliament were striving for mastery in the field, he was deciding their destinies in the closet. The weak and the credulous of both parties, who sought to be instructed in 'destiny's dark counsels,' flocked to consult the 'wily Archimage,' who, with exemplary impartiality, meted out victory and good fortune to his clients, according to the extent of their faith, and the weight of their purses. A few profane Cavaliers might make his name the burthen of their *malignant* rhymes—a few of the more scrupulous among the *Saints* might keep aloof in sanctified abhorrence of the 'Stygian sophister'—but the great majority of the people lent a willing and reverential ear to his prophecies and prognostications. Nothing was too high or too low—too mighty or too insignificant, for the grasp of his genius. The stars, his informants, were as communicative on the most trivial as on the most important sub-name was Robert Lilly, and died Vicar of Cambden in Gloucestershire, about 1640.

The town of Diseworth did formerly be-

jects. If a scheme was set on foot to rescue the king, or to retrieve a stray trinket—to restore the royal authority, or to make a frail damsel an honest woman—to cure the nation of anarchy, or a lap-dog of a surfeit, William Lilly was the oracle to be consulted. His *almanacks* were spelled over in the tavern and quoted in the senate; they nerved the arm of the soldier, and rounded the periods of the orator. The fashionable beauty, dashing along in her calash from St. James's or the Mall, and the prim, starched dame, from Watling-street or Bucklersbury, with a staid foot-boy, in a plush jerkin, plodding behind her—the reigning toast among ' the men of wit about town,' and the leading groaner in a tabernacle concert—glided alternately into the study of the trusty wizard, and poured into his attentive ear strange tales of love, or trade, or treason. The Roundhead stalked in at one door, whilst the Cavalier was hurried out at the other.

" The *Confessions* of a man so variously consulted and trusted, if written with the candour of a Cardan or a Rous-

long unto the Lord Seagrave, for there is one
record in the hands of my cousin Melborn
Williamson, which mentions one acre of land

seau, would indeed be invaluable.   The *Memoirs of William Lilly*, though deficient in this essential ingredient,
yet contain a variety of curious and interesting anecdotes
of himself and his cotemporaries, which, where the vanity
of the writer, or the truth of his art, is not concerned,
may be received with implicit credence.

" The simplicity and apparent candour of his narrative
might induce a hasty reader of this book to believe him a
well-meaning but somewhat silly personage, the dupe of
his own speculations—the deceiver of himself as well as
of others.   But an attentive examination of the events of
his life, even as recorded by himself, will not warrant so
favourable an interpretation.   His systematic and successful attention to his own interest—his dexterity in
keeping on 'the windy side of the law'—his perfect political pliability—and his presence of mind and fertility of
resources when entangled in difficulties—indicate an accomplished impostor, not a crazy enthusiast.   It is very
possible and probable, that, at the outset of his career, he

abutting north upon the gates of the Lord
Seagrave ; and there is one close, called
Hall-close, wherein the ruins of some ancient

was a real believer in the truth and lawfulness of his art,
and that he afterwards felt no inclination to part with so
pleasant and so profitable a delusion : like his patron,
Cromwell, whose early fanaticism subsided into hypocrisy,
he carefully retained his folly as a cloak for his knavery.
Of his success in deception, the present narrative exhi-
bits abundant proofs.   The number of his dupes was
not confined to the vulgar and illiterate, but included in-
dividuals of real worth and learning, of hostile parties and
sects, who courted his acquaintance and respected his
predictions.   His proceedings were deemed of sufficient
importance to be twice made the subject of a parliamentary
inquiry; and even after the Restoration—when a little
more scepticism, if not more wisdom, might have been expected—we find him examined by a Committee of the
House of Commons, respecting his fore-knowledge of the
great fire of London.   We know not whether it 'should
more move our anger or our mirth,' to see an assemblage
of British Senators—the cotemporaries of Hampden and

buildings appear, and particularly where
the dove-house stood; and there is also
the ruins of decayed fish-ponds and other
outhouses. This town came at length to be
the inheritance of Margaret, Countess of
Richmond, mother of Henry VII. which

Falkland—of Milton and Clarendon—in an age which
roused into action so many and such mighty energies—
gravely engaged in ascertaining the causes of a great na-
tional calamity, from the prescience of a knavish fortune-
teller, and puzzling their wisdoms to interpret the symbo-
lical flames, which blazed in the mis-shapen wood-cuts of
his oracular publications.

" As a set-off against these honours may be mentioned,
the virulent and unceasing attacks of almost all the party
scribblers of the day; but their abuse he shared in common with men, whose talents and virtues have outlived
the malice of their cotemporaries, and

‘Whose honours with increase of ages grow,
As streams roll down, enlarging as they flow.’ "

Retrospective Review, Vol. ii. p. 51.

Margaret gave this town and lordship of Diseworth unto Christ's College in Cambridge, the Master and Fellows whereof have ever since, and at present, enjoy and possess it.

In the church of this town there is but one monument, and that is a white marble stone, now almost broken to pieces, which was placed there by Robert Lilly, my grandfather, in memory of Jane his wife, the daughter of Mr. Poole of Dalby, in the same county, a family now quite extinguished. My grandmother's brother was Mr. Henry Poole, one of the Knights of Rhodes, or Templars, who being a soldier at Rhodes at the taking thereof by Solyman the Magnificent, and escaping with his life, came afterwards to England, and married the Lady Parron or Perham, of Oxfordshire, and was called, during his life, Sir Henry Poole. Wil-

liam Poole the Astrologer knew him very
well, and remembers him to have been a very
tall person, and reputed of great strength in
his younger years.

The impropriation of this town of Diseworth was formerly the inheritance of three
sisters, whereof two became votaries; one
in the nunnery of Langly in the parish of
Diseworth, valued at the suppression, I mean
the whole nunnery, at thirty-two pounds
per annum, and this sister's part is yet enjoyed by the family of the Grayes, who now,
and for some years past, have the enjoyment
and possession of all the lands formerly belonging to the nunnery in the parish of Diseworth, and are at present of the yearly value
of three hundred and fifty pounds per annum. One of the sisters gave her part of
the great tithes unto a religious house in
Bredon upon the Hill; and, as the inhabi-

tants report, became a religious person afterwards.

The third sister married, and her part of the tithes in succeeding ages became the Earl of Huntingdon's, who not many years since sold it to one of his servants.

The donation of the vicarage is in the gift of the Grayes of Langley, unto whom they pay yearly, (I mean unto the Vicar) as I am informed, six pounds per annum. Very lately some charitable citizens have purchased one-third portion of the tithes, and given it for a maintenance of a preaching minister, and it is now of the value of about fifty pounds per annum.

There have been two hermitages in this parish; the last hermit was well remembered by one Thomas Cooke, a very ancient inhabitant, who in my younger years acquainted me therewith.

This town of Diseworth is divided into three parishes; one part belongs under Locington, in which part standeth my father's house, over - against the west end of the steeple, in which I was born: some other farms are in the parish of Bredon, the rest in the parish of Diseworth.

In this town, but in the parish of Lockington, was I born, the first day of May 1602.

My father's name was William Lilly, son of Robert, the son of Robert, the son of Rowland, &c. My mother was Alice, the daughter of Edward Barham, of Fiskerton Mills, in Nottinghamshire, two miles from Newark upon Trent: this Edward Barham was born in Norwich, and well remembered the rebellion of Kett the Tanner, in the days of Edward VI.

Our family have continued many ages in this town as yeomen; besides the farm my

father and his ancestors lived in, both my
father and grandfather had much free land,
and many houses in the town, not belonging
to the college, as the farm wherein they were
all born doth, and is now at this present of
the value of forty pounds per annum, and in
possession of my brother's son; but the free-
hold land and houses, formerly purchased by
my ancestors, were all sold by my grandfather and father; so that now our family
depend wholly upon a college lease. Of my
infancy I can speak little, only I do remember that in the fourth year of my age I had
the measles.

I was, during my minority, put to learn at
such schools, and of such masters, as the
rudeness of the place and country afforded;
my mother intending I should be a scholar
from my infancy, seeing my father's back-
slidings in the world, and no hopes by plain

husbandry to recruit a decayed estate ;
therefore upon Trinity Tuesday, 1613, my
father had me to Ashby de la Zouch, to be
instructed by one Mr. John Brinsley ; one,
in those times, of great abilities for instruction of youth in the Latin and Greek tongues;
he was very severe in his life and conversation, and did breed up many scholars for the
universities: in religion he was a strict Puritan, not conformable wholly to the ceremo-
nies of the Church of England.   In this town
of Ashby de la Zouch, for many years together, Mr. Arthur Hildersham exercised his
ministry at my being there; and all the
while I continued at Ashby, he was silenced.
This is that famous Hildersham, who left
behind him a commentary on the fifty-first
psalm; as also many sermons upon the fourth
of John, both which are printed; he was
an excellent textuary, of exemplary life,

pleasant in discourse, a strong enemy to the
Brownists, and dissented not from the
Church of England in any article of faith,
but only about wearing the surplice, bap-
tizing with the cross, and kneeling at the
sacrament; most of the people in town were
directed by his judgement, and so continued,
and yet do continue presbyterianly affected;
for when the Lord of Loughborough in 1642,
1643, 1644, and 1645, had his garrison in
that town, if by chance at any time any
troops of horse had lodged within the town,
though they came late at night to their quar-
ters; yet would one or other of the town
presently give Sir John Gell of Derby notice,
so that ere next morning most of his Majesty's troops were seized in their lodgings,
which moved the Lord of Loughborough
merrily to say, there was not a fart let in
Ashby, but it was presently carried to Derby.

The several authors I there learned were these, viz. *Sententiæ Pueriles, Cato, Corderius, Æsop's Fables, Tully's Offices, Ovid de Tristibus;* lastly, *Virgil,* then *Horace;* as also *Camden's Greek Grammar, Theognis,* and *Homer's Iliads:* I was only entered into *Udall's Hebrew Grammar;* he never taught logick, but often would say it was fit to be learned in the universities.

In the fourteenth year of my age, by a fellow scholar of swarth, black complexion, I had like to have my right eye beaten out as we were at play; the same year, about Michaelmas, I got a surfeit, and thereupon a fever, by eating beech-nuts.

In the sixteenth year of my age I was exceedingly troubled in my dreams concerning my salvation and damnation, and also concerning the safety and destruction of the souls of my father and mother; in the nights

I frequently wept, prayed and mourned, for fear my sins might offend God.

In the seventeenth year of my age my mother died.

In the eighteenth year of my age my master Brinsley was enforced from keeping school, being persecuted by the Bishop's officers; he came to London, and then lectured in London, where he afterwards died. In this year, by reason of my father's poverty, I was also enforced to leave school, and so came to my father's house, where I lived in much penury for one year, and taught school one quarter of a year, until God's providence provided better for me.

For the two last years of my being at school, I was of the highest form in the school, and chiefest of that form; I could then speak Latin as well as English; could make extempore verses upon any theme;

all kinds of verses, hexameter, pentameter, phaleuciacks, iambicks, sapphicks, &c. so that if any scholars from remote schools came to dispute, I was ringleader to dispute with them; I could cap verses, &c. If any minister came to examine us, I was brought forth against him, nor would I argue with him unless in the Latin tongue, which I found few of them could well speak without breaking Priscian's head; which, if once they did, I would complain to my master, *Non bene intelligit linguam Latinam, nec prorsus loquitur.* In the derivation of words, I found most of them defective, nor indeed were any of them good grammarians: all and every of those scholars who were of my form and standing, went to Cambridge and proved excellent divines, only poor I, William Lilly, was not so happy; fortune then frowning upon father's present condition, he not in any capacity to maintain me at the university.

OF THE MANNER HOW I CAME UNTO LONDON.

Worthy sir, I take much delight to recount unto you, even all and every circumstance of my life, whether good, moderate, or evil; *Deo gloria.*

My father had one Samuel Smatty for his Attorney, unto whom I went sundry times with letters, who perceiving I was a scholar, and that I lived miserably in the country, losing my time, nor any ways likely to do better, if I continued there; pitying my condition, he sent word for me to come and speak with him, and told me that he had lately been at London, where there was a gentleman wanted a youth, to attend him and his wife, who could write, &c.

I acquainted my father with it, who was very willing to be rid of me, for I could not work, drive the plough, or endure any country labour; my father oft would say, I was good for nothing.

I had only twenty shillings, and no more, to buy me a new suit, hose, doublet, &c. my doublet was fustian: I repaired to Mr. Smatty, when I was accoutred, for a letter to my master, which he gave me.

Upon Monday, April 3, 1620, I departed from Diseworth, and came to Leicester: but I must acquaint you, that before I came away I visited my friends, amongst whom I had given me about ten shillings, which was a great comfort unto me. On Tuesday, April the 4th, I took leave of my father, then in Leicester gaol for debt, and came along with Bradshaw the carrier, the same person with whom many of the

Duke, of Buckingham's kindred had come up with. Hark how the waggons crack with their rich lading! It was a very stormy week, cold and uncomfortable: I footed it all along; we could not reach London until Palm-Sunday, the 9th of April, about half an hour after three in the afternoon, at which time we entered Smithfield. When I had gratified the carrier and his servants, I had seven shillings and sixpence left, and no more; one suit of cloaths upon my back, two shirts, three bands, one pair of shoes, and as many stockings. Upon the delivery of my letter my master entertained me, and next day bought me a new cloak, of which you may imagine (good Esquire) whether I was not proud of; besides, I saw and eat good white bread, contrary to our diet in Leicestershire. My master's name was Gilbert Wright, born at

Market Bosworth in Leicestershire; my mistress was born at Ashby de la Zouch, in the same county, and in the town where I had gone to school. This Gilbert Wright could neither write nor read: he lived upon his annual rents, was of no calling or profession; he had for many years been servant to the Lady Pawlet in Hertfordshire; and when Serjeant Puckering was made Lord keeper, he made him keeper of his lodgings at Whitehall. When Sir Thomas Egerton was made Lord Chancellor, he entertained him in the same place; and when he married a widow in Newgate Market, the Lord Chancellor recommended him to the company of Salters, London, to admit him into their company, and so they did, and my master in 1624, was master of that company; he was a man of excellent natural parts, and would speak publickly upon any occasion very rationally and to the purpose. I write this, that the world may know he was no taylor, or myself of that or any other calling or profession : my work was to go before my master to church ; to attend my master when he went abroad ; to make clean his shoes ; sweep the street ; help to drive bucks when he washed ; fetch water in a tub from the Thames : I have helped to carry eighteen tubs of water in one morning ; weed the garden ; all manner of drudgeries I willingly performed ; scrape trenchers, &c. If I had any profession, it was of this nature : I should never have denied being a taylor, had I been one ; for there is no calling so base, which by God's mercy may not afford a livelihood ; and had not my master entertained me, I would have been of a very mean profession ere I would have returned into the country again ; so here ends the actions of eighteen years of my life.

My master married his second wife for her estate; she was competently rich ; she married him for considerations he performed not, (nocturnal society) so that they lived very uncomfortably; she was about seventy years of age, he sixty-six or more ; yet never was any woman more jealous of a husband than she ; insomuch, that whensoever he went into London, she was confident of his going to women ; by those means my life was the more uncomfortable, it being very difficult to please two such opposite natures : however, as to the things of this world I had enough, and endured their discontents with much sereneness. My mistress was very curious to know of such as were then called cunning or wise

men, whether she should bury her husband?
She frequently visited such persons, and
this occasion begot in me a little desire to
learn something that way, but wanting
money to buy books, I laid aside these
motions, and endeavoured to please both
master and mistress.

OF MY MISTRESS'S DEATH, AND OCCASION THEREOF BY MEANS OF A CANCER IN HER BREAST.

In 1622 she complained of a pain in her
left breast, whereon there appeared at first
a hard knob no bigger than a small pea;
it increased in a little time very much, was
very hard, and sometimes would look very
red; she took advice of surgeons, had oils,
sear-cloths, plates of lead, and what not:
in 1623 it grew very big, and spread all

over her breast; then for many weeks
poultices were applied to it, which in continuance of time broke the skin, and then
abundance of watery thin stuff came from
it, but nothing else; at length the matter
came to suppuration, but never any great
store issued forth; it was exceeding noi-
some and painful; from the beginning of
it until she died, she would permit no
surgeon to dress it but only myself; I applied every thing unto it, and her pains
were so great the winter before she died,
that I have been called out of my bed two
or three times in one night to dress it and
change plaisters. In 1624 by degrees, with
scissars, I cut all the whole breast away,
I mean the sinews, nerves, &c. In one
fortnight, or little more, it appeared, as it
were, mere flesh, all raw, so that she could
scarce endure any unguent to be applied.

I remember there was a great cleft through the middle of the breast, which when that fully appeared she died, which was in September 1624; my master being then in the country, his kindred in London would willingly have had mourning for her; but by advice of an especial friend of his I contradicted them; nor would I permit them to look into any chest or trunk in the house. She was decently buried, and so fond of me in the time of her sickness, she would never permit me out of her chamber, gave me five pounds in old gold, and sent me unto a private trunk of her's at a friend's house, where she had one hundred pounds in gold; she bid me bring it away and take it, but when I opened the trunk I found nothing therein; for a kinsman of hers had been there a few days before, and carried all away: she was in a great passion at my relating thereof, because she could not gratify my pains in all her sickness, advised me to help myself, when she was gone, out of my master's goods, which I never did.

Courteous Esquire, be not weary of reading hereof, or what followeth.

When my mistress died, she had under her arm-hole a small scarlet bag full of many things, which, one that was there delivered unto me. There was in this bag several sigils, some of Jupiter in Trine, others of the nature of Venus, some of iron, and one of gold, of pure angel-gold, of the bigness of a thirty-three shilling piece of King James's coin. In the circumference on one side was engraven, *Vicit Leo de tribu Judæ Tetragrammaton* +, within the middle there was engraven a holy lamb. In the other circumference there was Amraphel and three +. In the middle, *Sanctus Petrus, Alpha* and *Omega.*

The occasion of framing this sigil was thus; her former husband travelling into Sussex, happened to lodge in an inn, and to lie in a chamber thereof; wherein, not many months before, a country grazier had lain, and in the night cut his own throat; after this night's lodging, he was perpetually, and for many years, followed by a spirit, which vocally and articulately provoked him to cut his throat: he was used frequently to say, 'I defy thee, I defy thee,' and to spit at the spirit; this spirit followed him many years, he not making any body acquainted with it; at last he grew melancholy and discontented; which being carefully observed by his wife, she many times hearing him pronounce, 'I defy thee,' &c. she desired him to acquaint her with the cause of his distemper, which he then did. Away she went to Dr. Simon Forman, who lived then in Lambeth, and acquaints him with it; who having framed this sigil, and hanged it about his neck, he wearing it continually untill he died, was never more molested by the spirit: I sold the sigil for thirty-two shillings, but transcribed the words *verbatim* as I have related. Sir, you shall now have a story of this Simon Forman, as his widow, whom I well knew, related it unto me. But before I relate his death, I shall acquaint you something of the man, as I have gathered them from some manuscripts of his own writing.

OF DR. SIMON FORMAN.

He was a chandler's son in the city of Westminster. He travelled into Holland for a month, in 1580, purposely to be instructed in astrology, and other more occult sciences; as also in physick, taking his degree of Doctor beyond seas: being sufficiently fur-

R.Cooper sculp!

nished and instructed with what he desired, he returned into England, towards the latter end of the reign of Queen Elizabeth, and flourished until that year of King James, wherein the Countess of Essex, the Earl of Somerset, and Sir Thomas Overbury's matters were questioned. He lived in Lambeth, with a very good report of the neighbourhood, especially of the poor, unto whom he was very charitable. He was a person that in horary questions (especially thefts) was very judicious and fortunate; so also in sicknesses, which indeed was his master-piece. In resolving questions about marriage he had good success: in other questions very moderate. He was a person of indefatigable pains. I have seen sometimes half one sheet of paper wrote of his judgment upon one question; in writing whereof he used much tautology, as you may see yourself, (most excellent Esquire) if you read a great book of Dr. Flood's, which you have, who had all that book from the manuscripts of Forman; for I have seen the same word for word in an English manuscript formerly belonging to Doctor Willoughby of Gloucestershire. Had Forman lived to have methodized his own papers, I doubt not but he would have advanced the Jatro-mathematical part thereof very completely; for he was very observant, and kept notes of the success of his judgments, as in many of his figures I have observed. I very well remember to have read, in one of his manuscripts, what followeth.

'Being in bed one morning,' (says he) 'I was desirous to know whether I should ever be a Lord, Earl, or Knight, &c. whereupon I set a figure; and thereupon my judgment:' by which he concluded, that within two years time he should be a Lord or great man:

'But,' says he, 'before the two years were expired, the Doctors put me in Newgate, and nothing came.' Not long after, he was desirous to know the same things concerning his honour or greatship. Another figure was set, and that promised him to be a great Lord within one year. But he sets down, that in that year he had no preferment at all; only 'I became acquainted with a merchant's wife, by whom I got well.' There is another figure concerning one Sir ——— Ayre his going into Turkey, whether it would be a good voyage or not: the Doctor repeats all his astrological reasons and musters them together, and then gave his judgment it would be a fortunate voyage. But under this figure he concludes, 'this proved not so, for he was taken prisoner by pirates ere he arrived in Turkey, and lost all.' He set several questions to know if he should attain the philo-

sophers' stone, and the figures, according to
his straining, did seem to signify as much;
and then he tuggs upon the aspects and configurations, and elected a fit time to begin
his operation; but, by and by, in conclusion,
he adds, 'so the work went very forward;
but upon the □ of ♂ the setting-glass broke,
and I lost all my pains:' he sets down five
or six such judgments, but still complains
all came to nothing, upon the malignant aspects of ♄ and ♂.   Although some of his astrological judgments did fail, more particularly those concerning himself, he being no
way capable of such preferment as he ambi-
tiously desired; yet I shall repeat some other
of his judgments, which did not fail, being
performed by conference with spirits.   My
mistress went once unto him, to know when
her husband, then in Cumberland, would
return, he having promised to be at home

near the time of the question; after some
consideration, he told her to this effect:
'Margery,' for so her name was, 'thy husband will not be at home these eighteen
days; his kindred have vexed him, and he
is come away from them in much anger: he
is now in Carlisle, and hath but three-pence
in his purse.' And when he came home he
confessed all to be true, and that upon leaving his kindred he had but three-pence in
his purse. I shall relate one story more, and
then his death.

One Coleman, clerk to Sir Thomas Beaumont of Leicestershire, having had some liberal favours both from his lady and her daughters, bragged of it, &c. The Knight brought
him into the star-chamber, had his servant
sentenced to be pilloried, whipped, and afterwards, during life, to be imprisoned. The
sentence was executed in London, and was

to be in Leicestershire: two keepers were
to convey Coleman from the Fleet to Leicester. My mistress taking consideration of
Coleman, and the miseries he was to suffer,
went presently to Forman, acquainted him
therewith; who, after consideration, swore
Coleman had lain both with mother and
daughters; and besides said, that the old
Lady being afflicted with fits of the mother,
called him into her chamber to hold down
the fits with his hands; and that he holding
his hands about the breast, she cried 'Lower,
lower,' and put his hands below her belly;
and then————He also told my mistress in
what posture he lay with the young ladies,
&c. and said, 'they intend in Leicester to
whip him to death; but I assure thee, Margery, he shall never come there; yet they
set forward to-morrow,' says he; and so his
two keepers did, Coleman's legs being locked

with an iron chain under the horse's belly.
In this nature they travelled the first and
second day; on the third day the two keepers, seeing their prisoner's civility the two
preceding days, did not lock his chain under
the horse's belly as formerly, but locked it
only to one side.   In this posture they rode
some miles beyond Northampton, when on
a sudden, one of the keepers had a necessity
to untruss, and so the other and Coleman
stood still; by and by the other keeper
desired Coleman to hold his horse, for he
had occasion also: Coleman immediately
took one of their swords, and ran through
two of the horses, killing them stark dead;
gets upon the other, with one of their swords;
'Farewell, gentlemen,' quoth he, 'tell my
master I have no mind to be whipped in Leicestershire,' and so went his way.   The two
keepers in all haste went to a gentleman's

house near at hand, complaining of their misfortune, and desired of him to pursue their prisoner, which he with much civility granted; but ere the horses could be got ready, the mistress of the house came down, and enquiring what the matter was, went to the stable, and commanded the horses to be unsaddled, with this sharp speech—'Let the Lady Beaumont and her daughters live honestly, none of my horses shall go forth upon this occasion.'

I could relate many such stories of his performances; as also what he wrote in a book left behind him, *viz.* 'This I made the devil write with his own hand in Lambeth Fields 1596, in June or July, as I now remember.' He professed to his wife there would be much trouble about Carr and the Countess of Essex, who frequently resorted unto him, and from whose company he would sometimes

lock himself in his study a whole day. Now
we come to his death, which happened as
follows: the Sunday night before he died,
his wife and he being at supper in their gar-
den-house, she being pleasant, told him,
that she had been informed he could resolve, whether man or wife should die first;
'Whether shall I' (quoth she) 'bury you or
no?' 'Oh Trunco,' for so he called her, 'thou
wilt bury me, but thou wilt much repent it.'
'Yea, but how long first?' 'I shall die,' said
he, 'ere Thursday night.' Monday came,
all was well. Tuesday came, he not sick.
Wednesday came, and still he was well;
with which his impertinent wife did much
twit him in his teeth. Thursday came, and
dinner was ended, he very well: he went
down to the water-side, and took a pair of
oars to go to some buildings he was in hand
with in Puddle-dock. Being in the middle

of the Thames, he presently fell down, only
saying, 'An impost, an impost,' and so died.
A most sad storm of wind immediately following. He died worth one thousand two
hundred pounds, and left only one son called Clement. All his rarities, secret manuscripts, of what quality soever, Dr. Napper
of Lindford in Buckinghamshire had, who
had been a long time his scholar; and of
whom Forman was used to say he would
be a dunce: yet in continuance of time he
proved a singular astrologer and physician.
Sir Richard now living, I believe, has all
those rarities in possession, which were
Forman's, being kinsman and heir unto Dr.
Napper. [His son Thomas Napper, Esq.;
most generously gave most of these manuscripts to Elias Ashmole, Esq.;] I hope you
will pardon this digression.

After my mistress was dead, I lived most

comfortably, my master having a great affection for me.

The year 1625 now comes on, and the plague exceeding violent, I will relate what I observed the spring before it broke forth. Against our corner house every night there would come down, about five or six of the clock, sometime one hundred or more boys, some playing, others as if in serious discourse, and just as it grew dark would all be gone home; many succeeding years there was no such, or any concourse, usually no more than four or five in a company: In the spring of 1625, the boys and youths of several parishes in like number appeared again, which I beholding, called Thomas Sanders, my landlord, and told him, that the youth and young boys of several parishes did in that nature assemble and play, in the bening of the year 1625. 'God bless us,' quoth

I, 'from a plague this year;' but then there
succeeded one, and the greatest that ever
was in London.   In 1625, the visitation
encreasing, and my master having a great
charge of money and plate, some of his own,
some other men's, left me and a fellow-servant to keep the house, and himself in June
went into Leicestershire. He was in that year
feoffee collector for twelve poor alms-people
living in Clement - Dane's Church - Yard ;
whose pensions I in his absence paid weekly,
to his and the parish's great satisfaction. My
master was no sooner gone down, but I
bought a bass-viol, and got a master to instruct me; the intervals of time I spent in
bowling in Lincoln's - Inn - Fields, with Wat
the cobler, Dick the blacksmith, and such
like companions: We have sometimes been
at our work at six in the morning, and so
continued till three or four in the afternoon,

many times without bread or drink all that
while. Sometimes I went to church and
heard funeral sermons, of which there was
then great plenty. At other times I went
early to St. Antholine's in London, where
there was every morning a sermon. The
most able people of the whole city and sub-
urbs were out of town; if any remained, it
were such as were engaged by parish-offi-
cers to remain; no habit of a gentleman or
woman continued; the woeful calamity of
that year was grievous, people dying in the
open fields and in open streets. At last, in
August, the bills of mortality so encreased,
that very few people had thoughts of sur-
viving the contagion: the Sunday before
the great bill came forth, which was of five
thousand and odd hundreds, there was appointed a sacrament at Clement Dane's;
during the destributing whereof I do very

well remember we sang thirteen parts of the one hundred and nineteenth Psalm. One Jacob, our minister (for we had three that day, the communion was so great) fell sick as he was giving the sacrament, went home, and was buried of the plague the Thursday following. Mr. James, another of the ministers, fell sick ere he had quite finished, had the plague, and was thirteen weeks ere he recovered. Mr. Whitacre, the last of the three, escaped not only then, but all the contagion following, without any sickness at all; though he officiated at every funeral, and buried all manner of people, 'whether they died of the plague or not. He was given to drink, seldom could preach more than one quarter of an hour at a time, &c. In November my master came home. My fellow - servant's and my diet came weekly to six shillings and sixpence, sometimes to seven shillings, so cheap was diet at that time.

In February of that year, my master married again (one who after his death became my wife.) In the same year he settled upon me, during my life, twenty pounds per annum, which I have enjoyed ever since, even to the writing hereof.

May 22, 1627, my master died at the corner house in the Strand, where I also lived so long. He died intestate; my mistress relinquishing the administration, it came to his elder brother, who assigned the estate over to me for payment of my master's debts; which being paid, I faithfully returned the remaining part unto his administrator; nor had one penny of the estate more than twenty pounds per annum, which was allowed me by contract, to undertake the payment of my master's debts.

E

OF MY MARRIAGE THE FIRST TIME.

My mistress, who had been twice married to old men, was now resolved to be couzened no more; she was of a brown ruddy complexion, corpulent, of but mean stature, plain, no education, yet a very provident person, and of good condition: she had many suitors, old men, whom she declined; some gentlemen of decayed fortunes, whom she liked not, for she was covetous and sparing: by my fellow-servant she was observed frequently to say, she cared not if she married a man that would love her, so that he had never a penny; and would ordinarily talk of me when she was in bed: this servant gave me encouragement to give the onset: I was much perplexed hereat, for should I attempt her, and be slighted,

she would never care for me afterwards; but
again, I considered that if I should attempt
and fail, she would never speak of it; or
would any believe I durst be so audacious
as to propound such a question, the dispro-
portion of years and fortune being so great
betwixt us: however, all her talk was of
husbands, and in my presence saying one
day after dinner, she respected not wealth,
but desired an honest man; I made answer,
I thought I could fit her with such a husband; she asked me, where? I made no
more ado, but presently saluted her, and
told her myself was the man: she replied, I
was too young; I said nay; what I had not
in wealth, I would supply in love; and
saluted her frequently, which she accepted
lovingly; and next day at dinner made me
sit down at dinner with my hat on my head,
and said, she intended to make me her hus-

band; for which I gave her many salutes,
&c.

I was very careful to keep all things secret,
for I well knew, if she should take counsel
of any friend, my hopes would be frustrated,
therefore I suddenly procured her consent to
marry, unto which she assented; so that
upon the eighth day of September, 1627, at
St. George's church in Southwark, I was
married unto her, and for two whole years
we kept it secret. When it was divulged,
and some people blamed her for it, she constantly replied, that she had no kindred; if
I proved kind, and a good husband, she
would make me a man; if I proved otherwise, she only undid herself. In the third
and fourth years after our marriage, we had
strong suits of law with her first husband's
kindred, but overthrew them in the end.
During all the time of her life, which was

until October, 1633, we lived very lovingly,
I frequenting no company at all; my exer-
cises were sometimes angling, in which I
ever delighted: my companions, two aged
men. I then frequented lectures, two or
three in a week; I heard Mr. Sute in Lom-
bard-Street, Mr. Gouge of Black-Fryars,
Dr. Micklethwait of the Temple, Dr. Olds-
worth, with others, the most learned men of
these times, and leaned in judgment to
Puritanism. In October, 1627, I was made
free of the Salters' company in London.

HOW I CAME TO STUDY ASTROLOGY.

It happened on one Sunday, 1632, as myself and a Justice of Peace's clerk were, before service, discoursing of many things, he
chanced to say, that such a person was a
great scholar, nay, so learned, that he could

make an Almanack, which to me then was strange : one speech begot another, till, at last, he said, he could bring me acquainted with one Evans in Gunpowder-Alley, who had formerly lived in Staffordshire, that was an excellent wise man, and studied the Black Art. The same week after we went to see Mr. Evans. When we came to his house, he, having been drunk the night before, was upon his bed, if it be lawful to call that a bed whereon he then lay; he roused up himself, and, after some compliments, he was content to instruct me in astrology; I attended his best opportunities for seven or eight weeks, in which time I could set a figure perfectly: books he had not any, except *Haly de judiciis Astrorum*, and *Origanus's Ephemerides ;* so that as often as I entered his house, I thought I was in the wilderness. Now something of the man: he was by birth a Welshman, a Master of Arts, and in sacred orders; he had formerly had a cure of souls in Staffordshire, but now was come to try his fortunes at London, being in a manner enforced to fly for some offences very scandalous, committed by him in these parts, where he had lately lived; for he gave judgment upon things lost, the only shame of astrology: he was the most saturnine person my eyes ever beheld, either before I practised or since; of a middle stature, broad forehead, beetle-browed, thick shoulders, flat nosed, full lips, down-looked, black curling stiff hair, splay-footed; to give him his right, he had the most piercing judgment naturally upon a figure of theft, and many other questions, that I ever met withal; yet for money he would willingly give contrary judgments, was much addicted to debauchery, and then very abusive and quarrel-

some, seldom without a black eye, or one
mischief or other: this is the same Evans
who made so many antimonial cups, upon
the sale whereof he principally subsisted;
he understood Latin very well, the Greek
tongue not at all: he had some arts above,
and beyond astrology, for he was well versed
in the nature of spirits, and had many times
used the circular way of invocating, as in
the time of our familiarity he told me. Two
of his actions I will relate, as to me delivered. There was in Staffordshire a young
gentlewoman that had, for her preferment,
married an aged rich person, who was desirous to purchase some lands for his wife's
maintenance; but this young gentlewoman,
his wife, was desired to buy the land in the
name of a gentleman, her very dear friend,
but for her use: after the aged man was
dead, the widow could by no means procure

the deed of purchase from her friend; where-upon she applies herself to Evans, who, for a sum of money, promises to have her deed safely delivered into her own hands; the sum was forty pounds. Evans applies himself to the invocation of the angel Salmon, of the nature of Mars, reads his Litany in the *Common-Prayer-Book* every day, at select hours, wears his surplice, lives orderly all that time; at the fortnight's end Salmon appeared, and having received his commands what to do, in a small time returns with the very deed desired, lays it down gently upon a table where a white cloth was spread, and then, being dismissed, vanished. The deed was, by the gentleman who formerly kept it, placed among many other of his evidences in a large wooden chest, and in a chamber at one end of the house; but upon Salmon's removing and bringing away the

deed, all that bay of building was quite blown
down, and all his own proper evidences torn
all to pieces.   The second story followeth.

Some time before I became acquainted
with him, he then living in the Minories, was
desired by the Lord Bothwell and Sir Kenelm
Digby to show them a spirit.   He promised
so to do: the time came, and they were all
in the body of the circle, when lo, upon a
sudden, after some time of invocation, Evans
was taken from out the room, and carried into the field near Battersea Causeway, close
to the Thames.   Next morning a countryman
going by to his labour, and espying a man
in black cloaths, came unto him and awaked
him, and asked him how he came there?
Evans by this understood his condition, enquired where he was, how far from London,
and in what parish he was ; which when he
understood, he told the labourer he had been

late at Battersea the night before, and by chance was left there by his friends. Sir Kenelm Digby and the Lord Bothwell went home without any harm, and came next day to hear what was become of him; just as they, in the afternoon, came into the house, a messenger came from Evans to his wife, to come to him at Battersea. I enquired upon what account the spirit carried him away: who said, he had not, at the time of invocation, made any suffumigation, at which the spirits were vexed. It happened, that after I discerned what astrology was, I went weekly into Little Britain, and bought many books  of astrology, not acquainting Evans therewith. Mr. A. Bedwell, Minister of Tottenham-High-Cross near London, who had been many years chaplain to Sir Henry Wotton, whilst he was Ambassador at Venice, and assisted Pietro Soave Polano, in composing

and writing the Council of Trent, was lately
dead; and his library being sold into Little
Britain, I bought amongst them my choicest
books of astrology. The occasion of our
falling out was thus: a woman demanded the
resolution of a question, which when he had
done, she went her way; I standing by all
the while, and observing the figure, asked
him why he gave the judgment he did, since
the signification shewed quite the contrary,
and gave him my reasons; which when he
had pondered, he called me boy, and must he
be contradicted by such a novice! But when
his heat was over, he said, had he not so
judged to please the woman, she would have
given him nothing, and he had a wife and family to provide for; upon this we never came
together after. Being now very meanly introduced, I applied myself to study those
books I had obtained, many times twelve, or

fifteen, or eighteen hours day and night; I was curious to discover, whether there was any verity in the art or not. Astrology in this time, viz. in 1633, was very rare in London, few professing it that understood any thing thereof. Let it not repent you (O noble Esquire) if now I make a short digression of such persons as then professed astrology, that posterity may understand in what condition I found it, and in whose hands that little that remained was lodged.

There lived then in Houndsditch one Alexander Hart, who had been a soldier formerly, a comely old man, of good aspect; he professed questionary astrology, and a little of physick; his greatest skill was to elect young gentlemen fit times to play at dice, that they might win or get money. I went unto him for resolutions for three questions at several times, and he erred in every one.

To speak soberly of him, he was but a cheat, as appeared suddenly after ; for a rustical fellow of the city, desirous of knowledge, contracted with Hart to assist for a conference with a spirit, and paid him twenty pounds of thirty pounds the contract. At last, after many delays, and no spirit appearing, or money returned, the young man indicts him for a cheat at the Old Bailey in London ; the Jury found the bill, and at the hearing of the cause this jest happened : some of the bench enquired what Hart did? ' He sat like an Alderman in his gown,' quoth the fellow; at which the court fell into a great laughter, most of the court being Aldermen. He was to have been set upon the pillory for this cheat; but John Taylour, the Water Poet, being his great friend, got the Lord Chief Justice Richardson to bail him, ere he stood upon the pillory, and so Hart fled presently into Holland, where he ended his days. It was my fortune, upon the sale of his books in 1634, to buy *Argoll's Primum Mobile* for fourteen shillings, which I only wanted.

In Lambeth Marsh at the same time lived one Captain Bubb, who resolved horary questions astrologically; a proper handsome man, well spoken, but withal covetous, and of no honesty, as will appear by this story, for which he stood upon the pillory. A certain butcher was robbed, going to a fair, of forty pounds; he goes to Bubb, who for ten pounds in hand paid, would help him to the thief; appoints the butcher such a night precisely, to watch at such a place, and the thief should come thither; commanded him by any means to stop him; the butcher attends according to direction. About twelve in the night there comes one riding very fiercely upon a full gallop, whom the butcher knocks

down, and seized both upon man and horse:
the butcher brings the man and horse to the
next town, but then the person whom the
butcher attacked was John the servant of Dr.
Bubb; for which the Captain was indicted
and suffered upon the pillory, and afterwards
ended his days in great disgrace.

There was also one Jeffry Neve, at this
time a student in physic and astrology; he
had formerly been a merchant in Yarmouth,
and Mayor of the town, but failing in estate,
went into the Low-Countries, and at Fra-
necker took the degree of Doctor in Physick; he had some little smattering in astrology; could resolve a question of theft, or
love-question, something of sickness; a very
grave person, laborious and honest, of tall
stature and comely feature; he died of late
years, almost in the very street near Tower-
Hill: he had a design of printing two hun-

dred verified questions, and desired my approbation ere they went to press; that I first would see them, and then give testimony. When I had perused the first forty, I corrected thirty of them, would read over no more: I showed him how erroneous they were, desired his emendation of the rest, which he performed not. These were afterwards, in R. Saunders's custody, bought by him either of his son or of a stationer.*

There was then William Poole, a nibbler at astrology, sometimes a gardener, an apparitor, a drawer of linen; as quoifs, handkerchiefs; a plaisterer and a bricklayer; he would brag many times he had been of seventeen professions; was very good company for drolling, as you yourself very well re-

---

* But first offered to be sold to me for twenty shillings. When Mr. Saunders died I bought them of his son for less. E. A——.

member (most honoured Sir);* he pretended
to poetry; and that posterity may have a
taste of it, you shall have here inserted two
verses of his own making; the occasion of
making them was thus. One Sir Thomas
Jay, a Justice of the Peace in Rosemary-
Lane, issued out his warrant for the apprehension of Poole, upon a pretended sugges-
tion, that he was in company with some lewd
people in a tavern, where a silver cup was
lost, *Anglice* stolen. Poole, hearing of the
warrant, packs up his little trunk of books,
being all his library, and runs to Westminster; but hearing some months after that the
Justice was dead and buried, he came and
enquired where the grave was; and after the
discharge of his belly upon the grave, left

* December 17, this William Poole was married to
Alice How, at St. George's Church in Southwark. Mr.
Lilly gave her to him.

these two verses upon it, which he swore he made himself.

Here lieth buried Sir Thomas Jay, Knight,
Who being dead, I upon his grave did write.

He died about 1651, or 1652, at St. Mary Overy's in Southwark; and this was part of his last will.

' Item; I give to Dr. Ardee all my books, and one manuscript of my own, worth one hundred of Lilly's Introduction.'

'Item; If Dr. Ardee give my wife any thing that is mine, I wish the devil may fetch him body and soul.' The Doctor, terrified with this curse, gave me all the books and his goods which I presently gave to his widow.—*Interdum seria jocis.*

Now also lived this Dr. Ardee, but his true name was Richard Delahay, formerly an Attorney; he studied astrology and physick, being in necessity, and forced from Derby-shire, where he had lived, by the old Countess of Shrewsbury; he was of moderate judgment, both in astrology and physick. He had formerly been well acquainted with Charles Sledd,* an apothecary, who used the crystal, and had a very perfect sight. This Dr. Ardee hath many times affirmed unto me, (*esto fides*) that an angel, one time, appeared unto him, and offered him a lease of his life for one thousand years; he died about the age of fourscore years; left his widow, who married into Kent,† worth two or three thousand pounds, and William Poole's estate came to four or five pounds.

In the years 1632 and 1633, John Booker became famous for a prediction of his upon a

---

* Of this Charles Sledd, there is mention made in Dr. Dee's book of his discourse with spirits, set forth by Dr. Casaubon.

† To one Moreland.

R. Cooper sculp.t

JOHN BOOKER.

From a rare Print by Hollar

PUBLISHED BY CHARLES HENRY BALDWYN NEWGATE STREET

solar eclipse in the 19th degree of Aries 1663, taken out of *Leovitius de magnis conjunctionibus,* viz. *Oh Reges et Principes &c.* Both the King of Bohemia, and Gustavus King of Sweden, dying during the effects of that eclipse.

John Booker was born in Manchester, of good parentage, in the year 1601; was in his youth well instructed in the Latin tongue, which he understood very well. He seemed from his infancy to be designed for astrology; for from the time he had any understanding, he would be always poring on, and studying almanacks. He came to London at fitting years, and served an apprenticeship to an haberdasher in Laurence-Lane, London; but either wanting stock to set up, or disliking the calling, he left his trade, and taught to write at Hadley in Middlesex several scholars in that school: he wrote singularly well both

Secretary and Roman. In process of time
he served Sir Christopher Clethero, Knight,
Alderman of London, as his clerk, being a
city Justice of Peace: he also was clerk to
Sir Hugh Hammersley, Alderman of London,
both which he served with great credit and
estimation; and by that means became not
only well known, but as well respected of
the most eminent citizens of London, even to
his dying day.

He was an excellent proficient in astrology, whose excellent verses upon the twelve
months, framed according to the configurations of each month, being blessed with success according to his predictions, procured
him much reputation all over England : he
was a very honest man, abhorred any deceit
in the art he studied ; had a curious fancy in
judging of thefts, and as successful in resolving love-questions : he was no mean pro-

ficient in astronomy; he understood much of physick; was a great admirer of the antimonial cup; not unlearned in chymistry, which he loved well, but did not practise. He was inclined to a diabetes; and in the last three years of his life was afflicted with a dysentery, which at last consumed him to nothing: he died of good fame in 1667. Since his decease I have seen one nativity of his performance exactly directed, and judged with as much learning as from astrology can be expected.

His library of books came short of the world's approbation, and were by his widow sold to Elias Ashmole, Esq. who most generously gave her * far more money than they were worth; but out of his respects unto the deceased and his memory, he most willingly

* They cost me one hundred and forty pounds.

paid her the money. He left behind him
two sons and two daughters. He left in
writing very little but his annual prognostications. He began first to write about the
year 1630; he wrote *Bellum Hibernicale*, in
the time of the long parliament, a very sober
and judicious book: the epistle thereunto I
gave him. He wrote lately a small treatise
of Easter-Day, a very learned thing, wherein
he shewed much learning and reading. To
say no more of him, he lived an honest man,
his fame not questioned at his death.

In this year 1633, I became acquainted
with Nicholas Fiske, licentiate in physick,
who was born in Suffolk, near Framingham*
Castle, of very good parentage, who educated him at country schools, until he was fit
for the university; but he went not to the

* There is no such place in Suffolk, it being mistaken
for Framlingham in that county.

academy, studying at home both astrology
and physick, which he afterwards practised
in Colchester; and there was well acquainted with Dr. Gilbert, who wrote *De Magnete*.
He came afterwards unto London, and exercised his faculty in several places thereof.
(For in his youth he would never stay long
in one house.) In 1633 he was sent for out
of Suffolk by Dr. Winston of Gresham College, to instruct the Lord Treasurer Weston's
son in arithmetick, astronomy upon the
globes, and their uses. He was a person
very studious, laborious, of good apprehension, and had by his own industry obtained
both in astrology, physick, arithmetick, astronomy, geometry and algebra, singular
judgment: he would in astrology resolve
horary questions very soundly; but was ever
diffident of his own abilities.: he was exquisitely skilful in the art of directions upon

nativities, and had a good genius in performing judgment thereupon, but very unhappy
he was, that he had no genius in teaching his
scholars, for he never perfected any: his
own son Matthew hath often told me, that
where his father did teach any scholars in
his time, they would principally learn of
him; he had Scorpio ascending, and was
secretly envious to those he thought had
more parts than himself; however, I must be
ingenuous, and do affirm, that by frequent
conversation with him, I came to know which
were the best authors, and much to enlarge
my judgment, especially in the art of directions: he visited me most days once after I
became acquainted with him, and would
communicate his most doubtful questions unto me, and accept of my judgment therein
rather than his own: he singularly well
judged and directed Sir Robert Holborn's

nativity, but desired me to adjudge the first house, seventh and tenth thereof, which I did, and which nativity (since Sir Robert gave it me) came to your hands, and remains in your library; [oh learned Esquire!] he died about the seventy-eighth year of his age, poor.

In this year also William Bredon, parson or vicar of Thornton in Buckinghamshire, was living, a profound divine, but absolutely the most polite person for nativities in that age, strictly adhering to Ptolemy, which he well understood; he had a hand in composing Sir Christopher Heydon's *Defence of Judicial Astrology*, being that time his chaplain; he was so given over to tobacco and drink, that when he had no tobacco, he would cut the bell-ropes and smoke them.

I come now to continue the story of my own life, but thought it not inconvenient to commit unto memory something concerning those persons who practised when first I became a student in astrology; I have wrote nothing concerning any of them, which I myself do not either know, or believe to be true.

In October 1633 my first wife died, and left me whatever was hers: it was considerable, very near to the value of one thousand pounds.

One whole year and more I continued a widower, and followed my studies very hard; during which time a scholar pawned unto me, for forty shillings, *Ars Notoria*,* a large volume wrote in parchment, with the names of those angels, and their pictures, which are thought and believed by wise men, to teach and instruct in all the several

---

* Among Dr. Napier's MSS. I had an *Ars Notoria*, written by S. Forman in large vellum.

liberal sciences, and is attained by observing elected times, and those prayers appropriated unto the several angels.

I do ingenuously acknowledge, I used those prayers according to the form and direction prescribed for some weeks, using the word *astrologia* for *astronomia;* but of this no more: that *Ars Notoria,* inserted in the latter end of Cornelius Agrippa signifieth nothing; many of the prayers being not the same, nor is the direction to these prayers any thing considerable.

In the year 1634, I taught Sir George Peckham, Knight, astrology, that part which concerns sickness, wherein he so profited, that in two or three months he would give a very true discovery of any disease, only by his figures. He practised in Nottingham, but unfortunately died in 1635, at St. Winifred's Well in Wales; in which well he continued

so long mumbling his *Pater Nosters* and
Sancta Winifrida ora pro me, that the cold
struck into his body; and, after his coming
forth of that well, never spoke more.

In this year 1634, I purchased the moiety
of thirteen houses in the Strand for five hundred and thirty pounds.

In November, the 18th day, I was again
the second time married, and had five hundred pounds portion with that wife; she was
of the nature of Mars.

Two accidents happened to me in that
yeaɪ something memorable.

Davy Ramsey, his Majesty's clock-maker,
had been informed, that there was a great
quantity of treasure buried in the cloyster of
Westminster-Abbey; he acquaints Dean
Williams therewith, who was also then Bishop of Lincoln; the Dean gave him liberty
to search after it, with this proviso, that if

any was discovered, his church should have a share of it. Davy Ramsey finds out one John Scott,* who pretended the use of the Mosaical rods, to assist him herein : I was desired to join with him, unto which I consented. One winter's night, Davy Ramsey, with several gentlemen, myself, and Scott, entered the cloysters ; we played the hazel-rod round about the cloyster; upon the west-side of the cloysters the rods turned one over another, an argument that the treasure was there. The labourers digged at least six foot deep, and then we met with a coffin; but in regard it was not heavy, we did not open, which we afterwards much repented. From the cloysters we went into the Abbey church, where, upon a sudden, (there being no wind when we began) so fierce, so high, so bluster-

* This Scott lived in Pudding-Lane, and had some time been a page (or such like) to the Lord Norris.

ing and loud a wind did rise, that we verily
believed the west-end of the church would
have fallen upon us; our rods would not
move at all; the candles and torches, all but
one, were extinguished, or burned very
dimly.* John Scott, my partner, was amazed,
looked pale, knew not what to think or do,
until I gave directions and command to dismiss the dæmons; which when done, all was
quiet again, and each man returned unto his
lodging late, about twelve o'clock at night;
I could never since be induced to join with
any in such-like actions.

The true miscarriage of the business, was
by reason of so many people being present
at the operation; for there was about thirty,
some laughing, others deriding us; so that
if we had not dismissed the dæmons, I be-

* Davy Ramsey brought an half quartern sack to put
the treasure in.

lieve most part of the Abbey church had been blown down; secrecy and intelligent operators, with a strong confidence and knowledge of what they are doing, are best for this work.

In 1634, or 1635, a Lady living in Greenwich, who had tried all the known artists in London, but to no purpose, came weeping and lamenting her condition, which was this: she had permitted a young Lord to have the use of her body, till she was with child by him; after which time he could not or would not endure her sight, but commanded his lacquies and servants to keep his doors fast shut, lest she should get into his chamber; or if they chanced to see her near his lodging, to drive her away, which they several times had done. Her desire unto me was to assist her to see him, and then she should be content; whereupon I ordered, such

a day, such an hour of that day, to try
her fortune once more.   She obeyed;
and when she came to the King's Bench,
where the Lord there was imprisoned, the
outward door stood wide open: none speaking a word unto her, she went up stairs, no
body molesting her; she found the Lord's
chamber door wide open: he in bed, not a
servant to be heard or seen, so she was
pleased.   Three days after she came to acquaint me with her success, and then drew
out of her pocket a paper full of ratsbane,
which, had she not had admission unto him
that day I appointed, she would in a pint of
white wine have drank at the stair's foot
where the Lord lodged.   The like misfortune
befell her after that; when the Lord was out
of prison : then I ordered her such a day to
go and see a play at Salisbury-Court; which
she did, and within one quarter of an hour

the Lord came into the same box wherein she was. But I grew weary of such employments, and since have burned my books which instructed these curiosities : for after that I became melancholy, very much afflicted with the hypochondriack, growing lean and spare, and every day worse ; so that in the year 1635 my infirmity continuing, and my acquaintance increasing, I resolved to live in the country, and in March and April 1636 removed my goods unto Hersham, where I now live; and in May my person, where I continued until 1641, no notice being taken who, or what I was.

In the years 1637 and 1638, I had great lawsuits both in the Exchequer and Chancery, about a lease I had of the annual value of eighty pounds : I got the victory.

In the year 1640 I instructed John Humphreys, master of that art, in the study of astrology : upon this occasion, being at London, by accident in Fleet-Street, I met Dr. Percival Willoughby of Derby ; we were of old acquaintance, and he but by great chance lately come to town, we went to the Mitre-Tavern in Fleet-Street, where I sent for old Will Poole the astrologer, living then in Ram-Alley : being come to us, the Doctor produced a bill, set forth by a master of arts in Cambridge, intimating his abilities for resolving of all manner of questions astrologically.   The bill was shewed, and I wondering at it Poole made answer, he knew the man, and that he was a silly fool ; 'I, quoth he, 'can do more than he ; he sees me every day, he will be here by and by ;' and indeed he came into our room presently : Poole had, just as we came to him, set a figure, and then shewed it me, desiring my judgement ; which I refused, but desired the master of arts to judge first; he denied, so I gave mine, to the very great liking of Humphreys, who presently enquired, if I would teach him, and for what? I told him I was willing to teach, but would have one hundred pounds. I heard Poole, whilst I was judging the figure, whisper in Humphrey's ear, and swear I was the best in England. Staying three or four days in town, at last we contracted for forty pounds, for I could never be quiet from his solicitations; he invited me to supper, and before I had shewed him any thing, paid me thirty-five pounds. As we were at supper a client came to speak with him, and so up into his closet he went with his client; I called him in before he set his figure, or resolved the question, and instantly acquainted him how he should discover the moles or marks of his client: he set his figure, and presently discovers four moles the querent had; and was so overjoyed therewith, that he came tumbling down the stairs, crying, 'Four by G—, four by G—, I will not take one hundred pounds for this one rule.' In six weeks time, and tarrying with him three days in a week, he became a most judicious person.

This Humphreys was a laborious person, vain-glorious, loquacious, fool-hardy, desirous of all secrets which he knew not, insomuch that he would have given me two hundred pounds to have instructed him in some curiosities he was persuaded I had knowledge of, but, *Artis est celare artem*, especially to those who live not in the fear of God, or can be masters of their own counsels: he was in person and condition such another as that monster of ingratitude my *quondam* taylor, John Gadbury. After my refusal of teaching him, what he was not capable of, we grew strange, though I afforded him many civilities whenever he required it; for after the siege of Colchester he wrote a book against me, called *Anti Merlinus-Anglicus*, married a second wife, his first living in Cambridgeshire, then practised physick by a contrary name, having intentions to practise in Ireland; he went to Bristol, but there understanding the parliament's forces had reduced that kingdom, he came back to London, but durst not abide therein; but running from his second wife, who also had another husband, he went to sea, with intention for Barbadoes, but died by the way in his voyage. I had never seen John Booker at that time; and telling him one day I had a desire to see him, but first, ere I would speak with him, I would fit myself with my old rules, and rub up my astrology; for at that time [and this was 1640] I thought John Booker the greatest and most complete astrologer in the world. My scholar Humphreys presently made answer, 'Tutor, you need not pump for any of your former knowledge, John Booker is no such pumper; we met,' saith he, 'the other day, and I was too hard for him myself, upon judgment of three or four questions.' If all the transactions happening unto that my scholar were in one volume, they would transcend either *Guzman, Don Quixote, Lazarillo de Tormes,* or any other of the like nature I ever did see.

Having now in part recovered my health, being weary of the country, and perceiving there was money to be got in London, and thinking myself to be as sufficiently enabled in astrology as any I could meet with, I made it my business to repair thither; and so in September 1641 I did; where, in the years 1642 and 1643, I had great leisure to better my former knowledge: I then read over all

my books of astrology, over and over; had
very little or no practice at all : and whereas
formerly I could never endure to read *Valen-
tine Naibod's Commentary upon Alcabitius,*
now having seriously studied him, I found
him to be the profoundest author I ever
met with; him I traversed over day and
night, from whom I must acknowledge
to have advanced my judgment and
knowledge unto that height I soon after arrived at, or unto : a most rational author,
and the sharpest expositor of *Ptolemy* that
hath yet appeared. To exercise my genius,
I began to collect notes, and thought of
writing some little thing upon the ♂ of ♄ and
♃ then approaching : I had not wrote above
one sheet, and that very meanly, but James
Lord Galloway came to see me; and, by
chance, casting his eyes upon that rude
collection, he read it over, and so ap-

proved of it, yea, so encouraged me to proceed farther, that then, and after that time, I spent most of my time in composing thereof, and bringing it, in the end, into that method wherein it was printed 1644. I do seriously now profess, I had not the assistance of any person living, in the writing or composing thereof. Mr. Fiske sent me a small manuscript, which had been Sir Christopher Heydon's, who had wrote something of the conjunction of ♄ and ♃, 1603; out of which, to bring my method in order, I transcribed, in the beginning, five or six lines, and not any more, though that graceless fellow Gadbury wrote the contrary: but, *Semel et semper nebulo et mendax.* I did formerly write one treatise, in the year 1639, upon the eclipse of the sun, in the eleventh degree of Gemini, May 22, 1639: it consisted of six sheets of paper. But that manuscript I gave unto my most munificent patron and ever bountiful friend, William Pennington, of Muncaster in Cumberland, Esq., a wise and excellently learned person; who, from the year 1634, even till he died, continued unto me the most grateful person I ever was acquainted with. I became acquainted with him by means of Davy Ramsey.

Oh! most noble Esquire, let me now beg your pardon, if I digress for some small time, in commemorating his bounty unto me, and my requital of his friendship, by performing many things successfully for his advantage.

In 1639 he was made captain, and served his Majesty in his then wars against the Scots; during which time a farmer's daughter being delivered of a bastard, and hearing, by report, that he was slain, fathered the child upon him. Shortly after he returned, most woefully vexed to be thus abused, when

absent. The woman was countenanced by
some gentlemen of Cumberland, in this her
villany against him; so that, notwithstanding he had warrants to attach her body, he
could never discover her: but yet, hunting
her from one place to another, her friends
thought it most convenient to send her to
London, where she might be in most safety.
She came up to the city, and immediately I
had notice thereof, and the care of that matter was left unto me. I procured the Lord
Chief Justice Bramston's warrant, and had it
lying dormant by me. She had not been in
the city above one fortnight, but that I, going
casually to the clerk of the assizes' office for
Cumberland, saw there an handsome woman;
and hearing of her speak the northern tone, I
concluded she was the party I did so want.
I rounded the clerk in his ear, and told him
I would give him five shillings to hold the

woman in chat till I came again, for I had a writing concerned her. I hasted for my warrant, and a constable, and returned into the office, seized her person before the clerk of the assizes, who was very angry with me: it was then sessions at Old-Bayley, and neither Judge nor Justice to be found. At night we carried her before the Recorder, Gardner. It being Saturday at night, she, having no bail, was sent to Bridewell, where she remained till Monday. On Monday morning, at the Old-Bayley, she produced bail; but I desiring of the Recorder some time to enquire after the bail, whether they were sufficient, returned presently, and told him one of the bail was a prisoner in Ludgate, the other a very poor man. At which he was so vexed, that he sent her to Newgate, where she lay all that week, until she could please me with good sureties; which then

she did, and so was bound over to appear at
the next assizes in Cumberland; which she
did, and was there sentenced to be whipped,
and imprisoned one whole year.

This action infinitely pleased Mr. Pennington, who thought I could do wonders; and I
was most thankfully requited for it. All the
while of this scandalous business, do what
he could, he could not discover what persons
they were that supported her; but the woman's
father coming to town, I became acquainted
with him, by the name of Mr. Sute, merchant; invited him to a dinner; got George
Farmer with me; when we so plied him with
wine, he could neither see or feel. I paid
the reckoning, twenty-two shillings. But
next morning the poor man had never a
writing or letter in his pocket. I sent them
down to my friend, who thereby discovered
the plots of several gentlemen in the business;

R. Cooper sculp.

CHARLES the SECOND.

From an Original Picture in the Collection of the Dutchess of Dorset at Knowle.

after which, Mr. Sute returned to his old name again.

Mr. Pennington was a true royalist, whom Charles the Second made one of his Commissioners of Array for Cumberland. Having directions from me continually how matters did and would go betwixt the King and Parliament, he acted warily, and did but sign one only warrant of that nature, and then gave over. When the times of sequestrations came, one John Musgrave, the most bold and impudent fellow, and most active of all the north of England, and most malicious against my friend, had got this warrant under Mr. Pennington's hand into his custody; which affrighted my friend, and so it might, for it was cause enough of sequestration, and would have done it. Musgrave intending himself great matters out of his estate, I was made acquainted herewith. Mus-

grave being in London, by much ado, I got
acquainted with him, pretending myself a
bitter enemy against Pennington, whereat
he very heartily rejoiced; and so we appointed one night to meet at the Five Bells,
to compare notes; for I pretended much.
We did meet, and he very suddenly produced
upon the table all his papers, and withal, the
warrant of array unto which my friend had
set his hand; which when I saw, ' I marry,'
said I, ' this is his hand I will swear; now
have at all; come, the other cup, this warrant shall pay for all.' I observed where the
warrant lay upon the table, and, after some
time took occasion ignorantly to let the candle fall out, which whilst he went to light
again at the fire, I made sure of the warrant,
and put it into my boot; he never missing it
of eight or ten days; about which time, I
believe, it was above half way towards Cum-

berland, for I instantly sent it by the post, with this friendly caveat, ' *Sin no more.*' Musgrave durst not challenge me in those times, and so the business was ended very satisfactory to his friend, and no less to myself.

He was, besides, extremely abused by one Isaac Antrobus, parson of Egremond, a most evil liver, bold, and very rich; at last he procured a minister of that country, in hope of the parsonage, to article against him in London, before the committee of plundered ministers. I was once more invited to solicit against Antrobus, which I did upon three or more articles.

I. That Antrobus baptized a cock, and called him Peter.

II. He had knowledge of such a woman and of her daughter, *viz.* of both their bo-

H

dies, in as large a manner as ever of his own wife.

III. Being drunk, a woman took a cord and tied it about his privy members unto a manger in a stable.

IV. Being a continual drunkard.

V. He never preached, &c.

Antrobus was now become a great champion for the Parliament; but, at the day of hearing, I had procured abundance of my friends to be there; for the godly, as they termed themselves, sided with him; the present Master of the Rolls was Chairman that day, Sir Harbottle Grimston.

Who, hearing the foulness of the cause, was very much ashamed thereof. I remember Antrobus, being there, pleaded he was in his natural condition when he acted so ungraciously.

' What condition were you in,' said the Chairman, ' when you lay with mother and daughter ?'

' There is no proof of that,' saith he.

' None but your own confession,' said the Chairman, ' nor could any tell so well.'

' I am not given to drunkenness,' quoth he. ' He was so drunk within this fortnight,' quoth I, ' he reeled from one side of the street to the other; here is the witness to prove it:' who, presently, before the committee, being sworn, made it good, and named the place and street where he was drunk. So he was adjudged scandalous, and outed of his benefice, and our minister had the parsonage.

You cannot imagine how much the routing of this drunken parson pleased Mr. Pennington, who paid all charges munificently and thankfully.

But now follows the last and greatest kindness I ever did him. Notwithstanding the committee for sequestrations in Cumberland were his very good friends, yet the sub-sequestrators, of their own heads, and without order, and by strength of arms, secured his irons, his wood, and so much of his personal estate as was valued at seven thousand pounds. Now had I complaint upon complaint: would I suffer my old friend to be thus abused? it was in my power to free him from these villains.

I hereupon advised what was best to do, and was counselled to get Mr. Speaker Lenthall's letter to the sub-sequestrators, and command them to be obedient to the committee of the county.

Whereupon, I framed a letter myself, unto the sub-sequestrators directed, and with it, myself and Mr. Laurence Maydwell (whom yourself well knew) went to Mr. Speaker, unto whom we sufficiently related the stubbornness of the officers of Cumberland; their disobedience to the committee; and then shewed him the letter, which when he had read over, he most courteously signed, adding withal, that if they proceeded further in sequestring Mr. Pennington, he would command a Serjeant at Arms to bring them up to answer their contempts: I immediately posted that letter to my friend, which when the absurd fellows received, they delivered him possession of his goods again; and, for my pains, when he came to London, gave me one hundred pounds; he died in 1652, of a violent fever.   I did carefully, in 1642 and 1643, take notice of every grand action which happened betwixt King and Parliament, and did first then incline to believe, that as all sublunary affairs did depend upon superior causes, so there was a possibility of discovering them by the configurations of the superior bodies; in which way making some essays in those two years, I found encouragement to proceed further, which I did ; I perused the writings of the ancients, but therein they were silent, or gave no satisfaction; at last, I framed unto myself that method, which then and since I follow, which, I hope, in time may be more perfected by a more penetrating person than myself.

In 1643, I became familiarly known to Sir Bulstrode Whitlocke, a member of the House of Commons; he being sick, his urine was brought unto me by Mrs. Lisle,* wife to John

---

* She was afterwards beheaded at Winchester, for harbouring one Nelthrop, a rebel in the Duke of Monmouth's army 1685. She had made herself remarkable, by saying at the martyrdom of King Charles I, 1648,

Lisle, afterwards one of the keepers of the Great Seal; having set my figure, I returned answer, the sick for that time would recover, but by means of a surfeit would dangerously relapse within one month; which he did, by eating of trouts at Mr. Sand's house, near Leatherhead in Surrey. Then I went daily to visit him, Dr. Prideau despairing of his life; but I said there was no danger thereof, and that he would be sufficiently well in five or six weeks; and so he was.

In 1644, I published *Merlinus Anglicus Junior* about April. I had given one day the copy thereof unto the then Mr. Whitlocke, who by accident was reading thereof in the House of Commons: ere the Speaker took

' that her blood leaped within her to see the tyrant fall;' for this, when she fell into the state trap, she neither did nor could expect favour from any of that martyr's family.

the chair, one looked upon it, and so did
many, and got copies thereof; which when I
heard, I applied myself to John Booker to
license it, for then he was licenser of all ma-
thematical books; I had, to my knowledge,
never seen him before; he wondered at the
book, made many impertinent obliterations,
framed many objections, swore it was not
possible to distinguish betwixt King and Parliament; at last licensed it according to his
own fancy; I delivered it unto the printer,
who being an arch Presbyterian, had five of
the ministry to inspect it, who could make
nothing of it, but said it might be printed,
for in that I meddled not with their Dagon.
The first impression was sold in less than one
week; when I presented some to the members of Parliament, I complained of John
Booker the licenser, who had defaced my
book; they gave me order forthwith to re-

print it as I would, and let them know if any durst resist me in the reprinting, or adding what I thought fit; so the second time it came forth as I would have it.

I must confess, I now found my scholar Humphreys's words to be true concerning John Booker, whom at that time I found but moderately versed in astrology; nor could he take the circles of position of the planets, until in that year I instructed him. After my *Introduction* in 1647 became publick, he amended beyond measure, by study partly, and partly upon emulation to keep up his fame and reputation; so that since 1647, I have seen some nativities by him very judiciously performed. When the printer presented him with an *Introduction* of mine, as soon as they were forth of the press; ' I wish,' saith he, ' there was never another but this in England, conditionally I gave one hundred pounds for this.' After that time we were very great friends to his dying day.

In June, 1644, I published *Supernatural Sight;* and, indeed, if I could have procured the dull stationer to have been at charges to have cut the *icon* or form of that prodigious apparition, as I had drawn it forth, it would have given great satisfaction; however, the astrological judgment thereupon had its full event in every particular.

That year also I published the *White King's Prophecy,* of which there were sold in three days eighteen hundred, so that it was oft reprinted: I then made no commentary upon it.

In that year I printed the *Prophetical Merlin,* and had eight pounds for the copy.

I had then no farther intention to trouble the press any more, but Sir Richard Napper having received one of Captain Wharton's

R. Cooper sculp.

CHARLES THE FIRST.

From a Picture by Vandyck.

PUBLISHED BY CHARLES & HENRY BALDWYN, NEWGATE STREET.

Almanacks for 1645, under the name Naworth, he came unto me : 'Now, Lilly, you are met withal, see here what Naworth writes.' The words were, he called me 'an impudent senseless fellow, and by name William Lilly.'

Before that time, 1 was more Cavalier than Roundhead, and so taken notice of; but after that I engaged body and soul in the cause of Parliament, but still with much affection to his Majesty's person and unto monarchy, which I ever loved and approved beyond any government whatsoever; and you will find in this story many passages of civility which I did, and endeavoured to do, with the hazard of my life, for his Majesty : but God had ordered all his affairs and counsels to have no successes; as in the sequel will appear.

To vindicate my reputation, and to cry quittance with Naworth, against whom I was

highly incensed, to work I went again for
Anglicus, 1645; which as soon as finished I
got to the press, thinking every day one
month till it was publick: I therein made
use of the King's nativity, and finding that
his ascendant was approaching to the qua-
drature of Mars, about June, 1645, I gave
this unlucky judgment; 'If now we fight, a
victory stealeth upon us;' and so it did in
June, 1645, at Naseby, the most fatal overthrow he ever had.

In this year, 1645, I published a treatise
called the *Starry Messenger*, with an interpretation of three suns seen in London, 29th
May, 1644, being Charles the Second's birth-
day: in that book I also put forth an astrological judgment concerning the effects of a
solar eclipse, visible the 11th of August,
1645. Two days before its publishing, my
antagonist, Captain Wharton, having given

his astronomical judgment upon his Majesty's present march from Oxford; therein again fell foul against me and John Booker: Sir Samuel Luke, Governor of Newportpagnel, had the thing came to his garrison from Oxford, which presently was presented unto my view. I had but twelve hours, or thereabout, to answer it, which I did with such success as is incredible; and the printer printed both the *March* and my answer unto it, and produced it to sight, with my *Starry Messenger*, which came forth and was made publick the very day of the Parliament's great victory obtained against his Majesty in person at Naseby, under the conduct of the Lord Thomas Fairfax.

That book no sooner appeared, but within fourteen days complaint was made to the committee of examinations, Miles Corbet then being Chairman, my mortal enemy, he who after was hanged, drawn, and quartered, for being one of the King's Judges; he grants his warrant, and a messenger to the Serjeant at Arms seizeth my person. As I was going to Westminster with the messenger, I met Sir Philip Stapleton, Sir Christopher Wray, Mr. Denzil Hollis, Mr. Robert Reynolds, who, by great fortune, had the *Starry Messenger* sheet by sheet from me as it came from the press. They presently fell a smiling at me; ' Miles Corbet, Lilly, will punish thee soundly ; but fear nothing, we will dine, and make haste to be at the committee time enough to do the business;' and so they most honourably performed ; for they, as soon as they came, sat down, and put Mr. Reynolds purposely into the chair, and I was called in; but Corbet being not there, they bid me withdraw until he came ; which when he did, I was commanded to appear, and Corbet desired to give the cause of my being in restraint, and of the committee's order. Mr. Reynolds was purposely put into the chair, and continued till my business was over.

Corbet produced my *Anglicus* of 1645, and said there were many scandalous passages therein against the Commissioners of Excise in London. He produced one passage, which being openly read by himself, the whole committee adjudged it to signify the errors of sub-officers, but had no relation to the Commissioners themselves, which I affirmatively maintained to be the true meaning as the committee declared.

Then Corbet found out another dangerous place, as he thought, and the words were thus in the printed book—' In the name of the Father, Son, and Holy Ghost, will not the Excise pay the soldiers ?'

Corbet very ignorantly read, ' will not the

Eclipse pay soldiers?' at which the Committee fell heartily to laugh at him, and so he became silent.

There was a great many Parliament men there ; the chamber was full. ' Have you any more against Mr. Lilly?' cried the chairman.

' Yes,' saith the Sollicitor for the Excise, ' since his *Starry Messenger* came forth we had our house burnt, and the Commissioners pulled by their cloaks in the Exchange.' ' Pray, sir, when was this,' asked old Sir Robert Pye, ' that the house was burnt, and the Aldermen abused?' ' It was in such a week,' saith he. ' Mr. Lilly, when came the book forth?' ' The very day of Naseby fight,' answered Mr. Reynolds, ' nor needs he be ashamed of writing it : I had it daily as it came forth of the press : it was then found the house to be burnt, and the Aldermen abused, twelve days before the *Starry Messenger* came forth.' 'What a lying fellow art thou,' saith Sir Robert Pye, 'to abuse us so!' This he spoke to the Sollicitor. Then stood up one Bassell, a merchant: he inveighed bitterly against me, being a Presbyterian, and would have had my books burnt. 'You smell more of a citizen than a scholar,' replied Mr. Francis Drake. I was ordered to withdraw, and by and by was called in, and acquainted the committee did discharge me. But I cried with a loud voice, 'I was under a messenger;' whereupon the committee ordered him or the Serjeant at Arms not to take any fees; Mr. Reynolds saying, 'Literate men never pay any fees.'

But within one week after, I was likely to have had worse success, but that the before-named gentlemen stoutly befriended me. In my Epistle of the *Starry Messenger*, I had

I

been a little too plain with the committee of
Leicestershire; who thereof made complaint
unto Sir Arthur Hazelrigg, Knight for that
county; he was a furious person, and made
a motion in the House of Commons against
me, and the business was committed to that
committee, whereof Baron Rigby was chairman. A day was assigned to hear the matter; in the morning whereof, as I passed by
Mr. Pullen's shop in St. Paul's Church-yard,
Pullen bad 'God be with you,' and named
me by name. Mr. Selden being there, and
hearing my name, gave direction to call me
unto him, where he acquaints me with Hazelrigg's humour and malice towards me,
called for the *Starry Messenger*, and having
read over the words mentioning that committee, he asked me how I would answer
them? I related what I would have said,
but he contradicted me, and acquainted me

what to say, and how to answer. In the afternoon I went to appear, but there was no committee set, or would sit; for both Mr. Reynolds and Sir Philip Stapleton, and my other friends, had fully acquainted Baron Rigby with the business, and desired him not to call upon me until they appeared; for the matter and charge intended against me was very frivolous, and only presented by a cholerick person to please a company of clowns, meaning the committee of Leicester. Baron Rigby said, if it were so he would not meddle with the matter, but exceedingly desired to see me. Not long after he met Sir Arthur, and acquainting him what friends appeared for me, said, 'I will then prosecute him no further.'

All the ancient astrologers of England were much startled and confounded at my manner of writing, especially old Mr. William Hodges,

who lived near Wolverhampton in Staffordshire, and many others who understood astrology competently well, as they thought.
Hodges swore I did more by astrology than
he could by the crystal, and use thereof,
which indeed he understood as perfectly as
any one in England. He was a great royalist,
but could never hit any thing right for that
party, though he much desired it: he resolved questions astrologically; nativities he
meddled not with; in things of other nature,
which required more curiosity, he repaired
to the crystal: his angels were Raphael,
Gabriel, and Uriel: his life answered not in
holiness and sanctity to what it should, having to deal with those holy angels. Being
contemporary with me, I shall relate what
my partner John Scott, the same Scott as is
before-mentioned, affirmed of him. John
Scott was a little skilful in surgery and phy-

sick, so was Will Hodges, and had formerly been a school-master. Scott having some occasions into Staffordshire, addressed himself for a month or six weeks to Hodges, assisted him to dress his patients, let blood, &c. Being to return to London, he desired Hodges to shew him the person and feature of the woman he should marry. Hodges carries him into a field not far from his house, pulls out his crystal, bids Scott set his foot to his, and, after a while, wishes him to inspect the crystal, and observe what he saw there. 'I see,' saith Scott, a ruddy complexioned wench in a red waistcoat, drawing a can of beer.' 'She must be your wife,' said Hodges. 'You are mistaken, Sir,' said Scott. 'I am, so soon as I come to London, to marry a tall gentlewoman in the Old Bailey.' 'You must marry the red waistcoat,' said Hodges. Scott leaves the coun-

try, comes up to London, finds his gentlewoman married: two years after going into
Dover, in his return, he refreshed himself at
an inn in Canterbury, and as he came into
the hall, or first room thereof, he mistook
the room, and went into the buttery, where
he espied a maid, described by Hodges, as
before said, drawing a can of beer, &c. He
then more narrowly viewing her person and
habit, found her, in all parts, to be the same
Hodges had described; after which he became a suitor unto her, and was married
unto her; which woman I have often seen.
This Scott related unto me several times,
being a very honest person, and made great
conscience of what he spoke. Another story
of him is as followeth, which I had related
from a person which well knew the truth of
it.

A neighbour gentleman of Hodges lost his

horse; who having Hodges's advice for recovery of him, did again obtain him. Some
years after, in a frolick, he thought to abuse
him, acquainting a neighbour therewith, viz.
That he had formerly lost a horse, went to
Hodges, recovered him again, but saith it
was by chance; I might have had him without going unto him: 'Come, let's go, I will
now put a trick upon him; I will leave some
boy or other at the town's-end with my horse,
and then go to Hodges and enquire for him.'
He did so, gave his horse to a youth, with
orders to walk him till he returned. Away
he goes with his friend, salutes Mr. Hodges,
thanks him for his former courtesy, and now
desires the like, having lost a horse very
lately. Hodges, after some time of pausing,
said; 'Sir, your horse is lost, and never to
be recovered.' 'I thought what skill you
had,' replies the gallant, 'my horse is walk-

ing in a lane at the town's-end.' With that Hodges swore (as he was too much given unto that vice) 'your horse is gone, and you will never have him again.' The gentleman departed in great derision of Hodges, and went where he left his horse : when he came there, he found the boy fast asleep upon the ground, the horse gone, the boy's arm in the bridle.

He returns again to Hodges, desiring his aid, being sorry for his former abuse. Old Will swore like a devil, 'be gone, be gone; go look for your horse.' This business ended not so ; for the malicious man brought Hodges into the star-chamber, bound him over to the assizes, put Hodges to great ex-pences : but, by means of the Lord Dudley, if I remember aright, or some other person thereabouts, he overcame the gentleman, and was acquitted.

Besides this, a gentlewoman of my acquaintance, and of credit, in Leicestershire, having lost a pillion-cloth, a very new one, went to desire his judgment. He ordered her such a day to attend at Mountsorrel in Leicestershire, and about twelve o'clock she should see her pillion-cloth upon a horse, and a woman upon it. My friend attended the hour and place; it being told, she must needs warm herself well, and then enquired if any passengers had lately gone by the inn? Unto whom answer was made, there passed by whilst she was at the fire, about half an hour before, a man, and a woman behind him, on horse-back. Inquiring of what colour the pillion-cloth was of; it was answered, directly of the colour my friend's was: they pursued, but too late.

In those times, there lived one William Marsh in Dunstable, a man of godly life and

upright conversation, a Recusant.   By astrology he resolved thievish questions with great
success ; that was his utmost sole practice.
He was many times in trouble ; but by Dr.
Napper's interest with the Earl of Boling-
broke, Lord Wentworth, after Earl of Cleveland, he still continued his practice, the said
Earl not permitting any Justice of Peace to
vex him.

This man had only two books, *Guido* and
Haly bound together : he had so mumbled
and tumbled the leaves of both, that half one
side of every leaf was torn even to the middle.   I was familiar with him for many
years : he died about 1647.

A word or two of Dr. Napper, who lived
at Great Lindford in Buckinghamshire, was
parson, and had the advowson thereof.   He
descended of worshipful parents, and this
you must believe ; for when Dr. Napper's

brother, Sir Robert Napper, a Turkey merchant, was to be made a Baronet in King
James's reign, there was some dispute
whether he could prove himself a gentleman
for three or more descents. ' By my saul,'
saith King James, ' I will certify for Napper,
that he is of above three hundred years
standing in his family, all of them, by my
saul, gentlemen,' &c. However, their family
came into England in King Henry the
Eighth's time. The parson was Master of
Arts; but whether doctorated by degree or
courtesy, because of his profession, I know
not. Miscarrying one day in the pulpit, he
never after used it, but all his life-time kept
in his house some excellent scholar or other
to officiate for him, with allowance of a good
salary : he out-went Forman in physick and
holiness of life; cured the falling-sickness

perfectly by constellated rings, some diseases by amulets, &c.

A maid was much afflicted with the falling sickness, whose parents applied themselves unto him for cure: he framed her a constellated ring, upon wearing whereof, she recovered perfectly. Her parents acquainted some scrupulous divines with the cure of their daughter: 'The cure is done by inchantment,' say they. 'Cast away the ring, it's diabolical; God cannot bless you, if you do not cast the ring away.' The ring was cast into the well, whereupon the maid became epileptical as formerly, and endured much misery for a long time. At last her parents cleansed the well, and recovered the ring again; the maid wore it, and her fits took her no more. In this condition she was one year or two; which the Puritan ministers there adjoining hearing, never left off, till they procured her parents to cast the ring quite away ; which done, the fits return- ed in such violence, that they were enforced to apply to the Doctor again, relating at large the whole story, humbly imploring his once more assistance ; but he could not be procur- ed to do any thing, only said, those who des- pised God's mercies, were not capable or worthy of enjoying them.

I was with him in 1632, or 1633, upon oc- casion. He had me up into his library, be- ing excellently furnished with very choice books : there he prayed almost one hour ; he invocated several angels in his prayer, viz.* Michael, Gabriel, Raphael, Uriel, &c. We parted.

* The collect read on Michaelmas-day, seems to allow of praying to angels. At some times, upon great occa- sions, he had conference with Michael, but very rarely.

He instructed many ministers in astrology,
would lend them whole cloak-bags of books;
protected them from harm and violence, by
means of his power with the Earl of Boling-
broke.* He would confess my master Evans
knew more than himself in some things : and
some time before he died, he got his cousin
Sir Richard to set a figure to see when he
should die. Being brought him; ' Well,' he
said, ' the old man will live this winter, but in
the spring he will die ; welcome Lord Jesus,
thy will be done.' He had many enemies ·.
Cotta, Doctor of physick in Northampton,
wrote a sharp book of witchcraft, wherein,
obliquely, he bitterly inveighed against the
Doctor.

In 1646, I printed a collection of Prophecies, with the explanation and verification of

---

* Lord Wentworth, after Earl of Cleveland.

Aquila, or the *White King's Prophecy;* as also the nativities of Bishop Laud and Thomas Earl of Strafford, and a most learned speech by him intended to have been spoke upon the scaffold. In this year 1646, after a great consideration, and many importunities, I began to fix upon thoughts of an *Introduction unto Astrology*, which was very much wanting, and as earnestly longed for by many persons of quality. Something also much occasioned and hastened the impression, viz. the malevolent barking of Presbyterian ministers in their weekly sermons, reviling the professors thereof, and myself particularly by name.

Secondly, I thought it a duty incumbent upon me, to satisfy the whole kingdom of the lawfulness thereof, by framing a plain and easy method for any person but of indifferent capacity to learn the art, and instruct him-

self therein, without any other master than
my *Introduction ;* by which means, when
many understood it, I should have more part-
ners and assistants to contradict all and every
antagonist.

Thirdly, I found it best as unto point of
time, because many of the soldiers were
wholly for it, and many of the Independant
party ; and I had abundance of worthy men
in the House of Commons, my assured friends,
no lovers of Presbytery, which then were in
great esteem, and able to protect the art; for
should the Presbyterian party have prevailed, as they thought of nothing less than to
be Lords of all, I knew well they would have
silenced my pen annually, and committed the
Introduction unto everlasting silence.

Fourthly, I had something of conscience
touched my spirit, and much elevated my
conceptions, believing God had not bestow-

ed those abilities upon me, to bury them under a bushel; for though my education was
very mean, yet, by my continual industry,
and God's great mercy, I found myself capable to go forward with the work, and to commit the issue thereof unto Divine Providence.

I had a hard task in hand to begin the first
part hereof, and much labour I underwent to
methodize it as it is.

I ingenuously confess unto you (Arts' great
Mecænas, noble Esquire Ashmole,) no mortal man had any share in the composition or
ordering of the first part thereof, but my only
self. You are a person of great reading, yet
I well know you never found the least trace
thereof in any author yet extant.

In composing, contriving, ordering, and
framing thereof (viz. the first part) a great
part of that year was spent. I again perused
all, or most, authors I had, sometimes adding,

at other times diminishing, until at last I thought it worthy of the press. When I came to frame the second part thereof, having formerly collected out of many manuscripts, and exchanged rules with the most able professors I had acquaintance with, in transcribing those papers for impression, I found, upon a strict inquisition, those rules were, for the most part, defective; so that once more I had now a difficult labour to correct their deficiency, to new rectify them according to art; and lastly, considering the multiplicity of daily questions propounded unto me, it was as hard a labour as might be to transcribe the papers themselves with my own hand. The desire I had to benefit posterity and my country, at last overcame all difficulties; so that what I could not do in one year, I perfected early the next year, 1647; and then in that year, viz. 1647, I

finished the third book of * nativities,† during the composing whereof, for seven whole
weeks, I was shut up of the plague, burying
in that time two maid-servants thereof; yet
towards November that year, the Introduction, called by the name of *Christian Astrology*, was made publick. There being, in
those times, some smart difference between
the army and the Parliament, the head-quarters of the army were at Windsor, whither I
was carried with a coach and four horses,
and John Booker with me. We were welcome thither, and feasted in a garden where
General Fairfax lodged. We were brought

---

* The name of the person whose nativity is directed
and judged, is Mr. Thompson, whose father had been
some time an inn-keeper at the White-Hart in Newark.

† I devised the forms and fashions of the several
schemes. E. A.

to the General, who bid us kindly welcome
to Windsor; and, in effect, said thus much:

'That God had blessed the army with
many signal victories, and yet their work
was not finished. He hoped God would go
along with them until his work was done.
They sought not themselves, but the welfare
and tranquillity of the good people, and
whole nation; and, for that end, were resolved to sacrifice both their lives and their
own fortunes. As for the art we studied, he
hoped it was lawful and agreeable to God's
word: he understood it not; but doubted
not but we both feared God; and therefore
had a good opinion of us both.' Unto his
speech I presently made this reply:

'My Lord, I am glad to see you here at
this time.

'Certainly, both the people of God, and
all others of this nation, are very sensible of

God's mercy, love, and favour unto them, in directing the Parliament to nominate and elect you General of their armies, a person so religious, so valiant.

' The several unexpected victories obtained under your Excellency's conduct, will eternize the same unto all posterity.

' We are confident of God's going along with you and your army, until the great work for which he ordained you both, is fully perfected; which we hope will be the conquering and subversion of your's and the Parliament's enemies, and then a quiet settlement and firm peace over all the nation, unto God's glory, and full satisfaction of tender consciences.

' Sir, as for ourselves, we trust in God; and, as Christians, believe in him. We do not study any art but what is lawful, and consonant to the scriptures, fathers, and antiquity; which we humbly desire you to believe,' &c.

This ended, we departed, and went to visit Mr. Peters the minister, who lodged in the castle, whom we found reading an idle pamphlet come from London that morning. 'Lilly, thou art herein,' says he. 'Are not you there also?' I replied. 'Yes, that I am,' quoth he.—The words concerning me were these :

> From th' oracles of the Sibyls so silly,
> The curst predictions of William Lilly,
> And Dr. Sybbald's Shoe-lane Philly,
>   Good Lord, deliver me.

After much conference with Hugh Peters, and some private discourse betwixt us two, not to be divulged, we parted, and so came back to London.

King Charles the First, in the year 1646,

R.Cooper sculp!

HUGH PETERS.

From an original Picture.

PUBLISHED BY CHARLES&HENRY BALDWYN NEWGATE STREET.

April 27, went unto the Scots, then in this nation. Many desired my judgment, in time of his absence, to discover the way he might be taken : which I would never be drawn unto, or give any direction concerning his person.

There were many lewd Mercuries printed both in London and Oxford, wherein I was sufficiently abused, in this year, 1646. I had then my ascendant *ad* □ ♂, and ☾ *ad proprium*. The Presbyterians were, in their pulpits, as merciless as the Cavaliers in their pamphlets.

About this time, the most famous mathematician of all Europe,* Mr. William Oughtred, parson of Aldbury in Surry, was in dan-

---

* This gentleman I was very well acquainted with, having lived at the house over-against his, at Aldbury in Surrey, three or four years. E. A.

ger of sequestration by the Committee of or
for plundered ministers ; *(Ambo-dexters* they
were;) several inconsiderable articles were
deposed and sworn against him, material
enough to have sequestered him, but that,
upon his day of hearing, I applied myself to
Sir Bolstrode Whitlock, and all my own old
friends, who in such numbers appeared in
his behalf, that though the chairman and
many other Presbyterian members were stiff
against him, yet he was cleared by the major
number. The truth is, he had a considerable
parsonage, and that only was enough to se-
quester any moderate judgment: he was also
well known to affect his Majesty. In these
times many worthy ministers lost their livings
or benefices, for not complying with the
Three-penny Directory. Had you seen (O
noble Esquire) what pitiful ideots were pre-
fered into sequestrated church-benefices, you

would have been grieved in your soul; but when they came before the classis of divines, could those simpletons but only say, they were converted by hearing such a sermon, such a lecture, of that godly man Hugh Peters, Stephen Marshall, or any of that gang, he was presently admitted.

In 1647, I published the *World's Catastrophe*, the *Prophecies of Ambrose Merlin*, with the *Key* wherewith to unlock those obstruse Prophecies; also *Trithemius of the Government of the World by the presiding Angels;* these came forth all in one book.

The two first were exquisitely translated by yourself, (most learned Sir) as I do ingenuously acknowledge in my *Epistle unto the Reader*, with a true character of the worth and admirable parts, unto which I refer any that do desire to read you perfectly delineated. I was once resolved to have continued *Trithemius* for some succeeding years, but multiplicity of employment impeded me. The study required, in that kind of learning, must be sedentary, of great reading, sound judgment, which no man can accomplish except he wholly retire, use prayer, and ac- company himself with angelical consorts.

His Majesty Charles the First, having en- trusted the Scots with his person, was, for money, delivered into the hands of the Eng- lish Parliament, and, by several removals, was had to Hampton-Court, about July or August 1647 ; for he was there, and at that time when my house was visited with the plague. He was desirous to escape from the soldiery, and to obscure himself for some time near London, the citizens whereof began now to be unruly, and alienated in affection from the Parliament, inclining wholly to his Majesty, and very averse to the army. His

Majesty was well informed of all this, and thought to make good use hereof; besides, the army and Parliament were at some odds, who should be masters. Upon the King's intention to escape, and with his consent, Madam Whorewood (whom you knew very well, worthy Esquire) came to receive my judgment, viz. In what quarter of this nation he might be most safe, and not to be discovered until himself pleased.

When she came to my door, I told her I would not let her come into my house, for I buried a maid-servant of the plague very lately. ' I fear not the plague, but the pox,' quoth she; so up we went. After erection of my figure, I told her about twenty miles (or thereabouts) from London, and in Essex, I was certain he might continue undiscovered. She liked my judgment very well; and, being herself of a sharp judgment, remembered a place in Essex about that distance, where was an excellent house, and all conveniences for his reception. Away she went, early next morning, unto Hampton-Court, to acquaint his Majesty; but see the misfortune: He, either guided by his own approaching hard fate, or misguided by *Ashburnham, went away in the night-time westward, and surrendered himself to Hammond, in the Isle of Wight.

Whilst his Majesty was at Hampton-Court Alderman Adams sent his Majesty one thousand pounds in gold, five hundred whereof he gave Madam Whorewood. I believe I had twenty pieces of that very gold for my share.

* This Ashburnham was turned out of the House of Commons the 3d of November, 1667, for taking a bribe of five hundred pounds of the merchants. I was informed hereof 26th November, 1667.

I have something more to write of Charles the First's misfortunes, wherein I was concerned; the matter happened in 1648, but I thought good to insert it here, having after this no more occasion to mention him.

His Majesty being in Carisbrook-Castle in the Isle of Wight, the Kentish men, in great numbers, rose in arms, and joined with the Lord Goring; a considerable number of the best ships revolted from the Parliament; the citizens of London were forward to rise against the Parliament; his Majesty laid his design to escape out of prison, by sawing the iron bars of his chamber window; a small ship was provided, and anchored not far from the castle to bring him into Sussex; horses were provided ready to carry him through Sussex into Kent, so that he might be at the head of the army in Kent, and from thence to march immediately to London, where

thousands then would have armed for him.
The Lady Whorewood came to me, acquaints
me herewith.   I got G. Farmer (who was a
most ingenious lock-smith, and dwelt in Bow-
lane) to make a saw to cut the iron bars in
sunder, I mean to saw them, and aqua fortis
besides.   His Majesty in a small time did his
work; the bars gave liberty for him to go
out; he was out with his body till he came
to his breast; but then his heart failing, he
proceeded no farther: when this was discovered, as soon after it was, he was narrowly
looked after, and no opportunity after that
could be devised to enlarge him.   About September the Parliament sent their Commissioners with propositions unto him into the Isle
of Wight, the Lord William Sea being one;
the Lady Whorewood comes again unto me
from him or by his consent, to be directed:
After perusal of my figure, I told her the

Commissioners would be there such a day; I elected a day and hour when to receive the Commissioners and propositions; and as soon as the propositions were read, to sign them, and make haste with all speed to come up with the Commisioners to London. The army being then far distant from London, and the city enraged stoutly against them, he promised he would do so. That night the Commissioners came, and old Sea and his Majesty had private conference till one in the morning: the King acquaints Sea with his intention, who clearly dissuaded him from signing the propositions, telling him they were not fit for him to sign; that he had many friends in the House of Lords, and some in the House of Commons; that he would procure more, and then they would frame more easy propositions. This flattery of this unfortunate Lord occasioned his Majesty to

wave the advice I and some others that wish-
ed his prosperity had given, in expectation of
that which afterwards could never be gained.
The army having some notice hereof from one
of the Commissioners, who had an eye upon
old Sea, hasted unto London, and made the
citizens very quiet; and besides, the Parliament and army kept a better correspondency
afterwards with each other.

Whilst the King was at Windsor-Castle,
once walking upon the leads there, he looked
upon Captain Wharton's *Almanack :* ' My
book,' saith he, ' speaks well as to the wea-
ther :' One William Allen standing by ;
' what,' saith he, ' saith his antagonist, Mr.
Lilly ?' ' I do not care for Lilly,' said his
Majesty, ' he hath been always against me,'
and became a little bitter in his expressions.
' Sir,' saith Allen, ' the man is an honest
man, and writes but what his art informs

him.' ' I believe it,' said his Majesty, "and that Lilly understands astrology as well as any man in Europe.' *Exit Rex Carolus.*

In 1648 I published a *Treatise of the Three Suns,* seen the winter preceding; as also an Astrological Judgment upon a Conjunction of Saturn and Mars 28 June, in 11 degrees 8 minutes of Gemini.

I commend unto your perusal that book and the *Prophetical Merlin,* which, seriously considered, (Oh worthy Esquire) will more instruct your judgement *(De generalibus contingentibus Mundi)* than all the authors you yet ever met with.

In this year, for very great considerations, the Council of State gave me in money fifty pounds, and a pension of one hundred pounds *per Annum,* which for two years I received, but no more: upon some discontents I after would not or did require it. The cause moving them was this; they could get no intelligence out of France, although they had several agents there for that purpose. I had formerly acquaintance with a secular priest, at this time confessor to one of the Secretaries; unto him I wrote, and by that means had perfect knowledge of the chiefest concernments of France, at which they admired; but I never yet, until this day, revealed the name of the person.

One occasion why I deserted that employment was, because Scott, who had eight hundred pounds *per Annum* for intelligence, would not contribute any occasion to gratify my friend: And another thing was, I received some affront from Gualter Frost their Secretary, one that was a principal minister belonging to the Council of State. Scott was ever my enemy, the other knave died of a gangrene in his arm suddenly after.

In 1648 and 1649, that I might encourage young students in astrology, I publickly read over the first part of my *Introduction*, wherein there are many things contained, not easily to be understood.

And now we are entered into the year 1649 : his Majesty being at St. James's House, in January of that year, I begun its observations thus :

" I am serious, I beg and expect justice ; either fear or shame begins to question offenders.

" The lofty cedars begin to divine a thundering hurricane is at hand ; God elevates men contemptible.

" Our demigods are sensible we begin to dislike their actions very much in London, more in the country.

" Blessed be God, who encourages his servants, makes them valiant, and of undaunted spirits, to go on with his decrees: upon a sudden, great expectations arise, and men generally believe a quiet and calm time draws nigh."

In Christmas holidays, the Lord Gray of Grooby and Hugh Peters sent for me to Somerset-House, with directions to bring them two of my Almanacks.—I did so; Peters and he read January's Observations.

' If we are not fools and knaves,' saith he, ' we shall do justice:' then they whispered. I understood not their meaning till his Majesty was beheaded. They applied what I wrote of justice, to be understood of his Majesty, which was contrary to my intention; for Jupiter, the first day of January, became direct; and Libra is a sign signifying Justice; I implored for justice generally upon such as had cheated in their places, being treasurers, and such like officers. I had not then heard the

least intimation of bringing the King unto
trial, and yet the first day thereof I was casually there, it being upon a Saturday; for
going to Westminster every Saturday in the
afternoon, in these times, at White-hall I casually met Peters; ' Come, Lilly, wilt thou
go hear the King tried?' ' When?' said I.
' Now, just now; go with me.' I did so, and
was permitted by the guard of soldiers to
pass up to the King's-Bench. Within one
quarter of an hour came the Judges, presently his Majesty, who spoke excellently well,
and majestically, without impediment in the
least when he spoke. I saw the silver top
of his staff unexpectedly fall to the ground,
which was took up by Mr. Rushworth: and
then I heard Bradshaw the Judge say to his
Majesty,

' Sir, instead of answering the court, you

interrogate their power, which becomes not
one in your condition'—

These words pierced my heart and soul, to
hear a subject thus audaciously to reprehend
his Sovereign, who ever and anon replied
with great magnanimity and prudence.

After that his Majesty was beheaded, the
Parliament for some years effected nothing
either for the publick peace or tranquillity
of the nation, or settling religion as they had
formerly promised. The interval of time betwixt his Majesty's death and Oliver Crom-
wel's displacing them, was wholly consumed
in voting for themselves, and bringing their
own relations to be members of Parliament,
thinking to make a trade thereof.

The week, or three or four days before his
Majesty's beheading, one Major Sydenham,
who had commands in Scotland, came to

take his leave of me, and told me the King was to be put to death, which I was not willing to believe, and said, ' I could not be persuaded the Parliament could find any Englishman so barbarous, that would do that foul action.' ' Rather,' saith he, ' than they should want such a man, these arms of mine should do it.' He went presently after into Scotland, and upon the first engagement against them, was slain, and his body miserably cut and mangled.

In 1651 I published *Monarchy or no Monarchy*, and in the latter end thereof some hieroglyphics of my own, composed, at spare time, by the occult learning, many of those types having representations of what should from thence succeed in England, and have since had verification.

I had not that learning from books, or any manuscript I ever yet met withal, it is reduced from a cabal lodging in astrology, but so mysterious and difficult to be attained, that I have not yet been acquainted with any who had that knowledge. I will say no more thereof, but that the asterisms and signs and constellations give greatest light thereunto.

During Bradshaw's being President of the Council of State, it was my happiness to procure Captain Wharton his liberty, which when Bradshaw understood, said, ' I will be an enemy to Lilly, if ever he come before me.' Sir Bolstrode Whitlock broke the ice first of all on behalf of Captain Wharton: after him the Committee, unto whom his offence. had been committed, spoke for him, and said he might well be bailed or enlarged : I had spoken to the Committee the morning of his delivery, who thereupon were so civil unto him, especially Sir William Ermin of Lincolnshire, who at first wondered I appeared not against him; but upon my humble request, my long continued antagonist was enlarged and had his liberty.

In 1651 I purchased one hundred and ten pounds *per Annum* in fee-farm rents for one thousand and thirty pounds. I paid all in ready money; but when his Majesty King Charles the Second, 1660, was restored, I lost it all again, and it returned to the right owner; the loss thereof never afflicted me, for I have ever reduced my mind according to my fortune. I was drawn in by several persons to make that simple purchase. The year I bought it, I had my ascendant directed into a Trine of Jupiter first, and in the same year into the *Cauda Draconis*—my fortune into a quadrant of Mercury When Colchester was besieged, John Booker and myself were sent for, where we encouraged the soldiers, assuring them the town would very shortly be sur-

rendered, as indeed it was: I would willingly have obtained leave to enter the town, to
have informed Sir Charles Lucas, whom I
well knew, with the condition of affairs as
they then stood, he being deluded by false
intelligence: at that time my scholar Humphreys was therein, who many times deluded
the Governor with expectation of relief; but
failing very many times with his lies, at last
he had the bastinado, was put in prison, and
inforced to become a soldier; and well it was
he escaped so.—During my being there, the
steeple of St. Mary's Church was much bat-
tered by two cannons purposely placed: I
was there one day about three of the clock
in the afternoon, talking with the cannoneer,
when presently he desired us to look to ourselves, for he perceived by his perspective
glass there was a piece charged in the castle
against his work, and ready to be discharged.

I ran for haste under an old ash-tree, and immediately the cannon-bullet came hissing quite over us. ' No danger now,' saith the gunner, ' but begone, for there are five more charging,' which was true; for two hours after those cannons were discharged, and unluckily killed our cannoneer and matross. I came the next morning and saw the blood of the two poor men lie upon the planks: we were well entertained at the head-quarters, and after two whole days abiding there, came for London.

But we prosecute our story again, and say that in the year 1652 I purchased my house and some lands in Hersham, in the parish of Walton upon Thames, in the county of Surrey, where I now live; intending by the blessing of God, when I found it convenient, to retire into the country, there to end my days in peace and tranquillity; for in

London my practice was such, I had none or
very little time afforded me to serve God,
who had been so gracious unto me. The
purchase of the house and lands, and buildings, stood me in nine hundred and fifty
pounds sterling, which I have very much
augmented.

The Parliament now grows odious unto
all good men, the members whereof became
insufferable in their pride, covetousness, self-
ends, laziness, minding nothing but how to
enrich themselves. Much heart-burning now
arose betwixt the Presbyterian and Independant, the latter siding with the army,
betwixt whose two judgments there was no
medium. Now came up, or first appeared,
that monstrous people called Ranters: and
many other novel opinions, in themselves he-
retical and scandalous, were countenanced
by members of Parliament, many whereof

were of the same judgment. Justice was neglected, vice countenanced, and all care of the common good laid aside. Every judgment almost groaned under the heavy burthen they then suffered; the army neglected; the city of London scorned; the ministry, especially those who were orthodox and serious, honest or virtuous, had no countenance; my soul began to loath the very name of a Parliament, or Parliament-men. There yet remained in the House very able, judicious, and worthy patriots; but they, by their silence, only served themselves: all was carried on by a rabble of dunces, who being the greater number, voted what seemed best to their non-intelligent fancies.

In this year I published *Annus Tenebrosus*, which book I did not so entitle, because of the great obscurity of the solar eclipse, by so many prattled of to no purpose, but because

of those underhand and clandestine counsels
held in England by the soldiery, of which I
would never, but in generals, give any knowledge unto any Parliament man.   I had wrote
publickly in 1650, that the Parliament should
not continue, but a new government should
arise, &c.

In my next year's *Anglicus*, upon rational
grounds in astrology, I was so bold as to aver
therein, that the Parliament stood upon a
tottering foundation, and that the common-
alty and soldiery would join together against
them.

My *Anglicus* was for a whole week every
day in the Parliament House, peeped into
by the Presbyterians, one disliking this sentence, another finds another fault, others
misliked the whole; so in the end a motion
was made, that *Anglicus* should be inspected
by the Committee for plundered ministers;

R.Cooper sculp!

WILLIAM LENTHALL.

Speaker of the House of Commons.

From a Miniature by Cooper.

PUBLISHED BY CHARLES & HENRY BALDWYN, NEWGATE STREET

which being done, they were to return them to the House, viz. report its errors.

A messenger attached me by a warrant from that Committee; I had private notice ere the messenger came, and hasted unto Mr. Speaker Lenthall, ever my friend. He was exceeding glad to see me, told me what was done ; called for *Anglicus*, marked the passages which tormented the Presbyterians so highly. I presently sent for Mr. Warren the printer, an assured Cavalier, obliterated what was most offensive, put in other more significant words, and desired only to have six amended against next morning, which very honestly he brought me. I told him my design was to deny the book found fault with, to own only the six books. I told him, I doubted he would be examined. ‘ Hang them,’ said he, ‘ they are all rogues. I’ll

swear myself to the devil ere they shall have
an advantage against you by my oath.'

The day after, I appeared before the Committee, being thirty-six in number that day;
whereas it was observed, at other times, it was
very difficult to get five of them together. At
first they shewed me the true *Anglicus*, and
asked if I wrote and printed it. I took the
book and inspected it very heedfully; and
when I had done so, said thus:

'This is none of my book, some malicious
Presbyterian hath wrote it, who are my mortal enemies; I disown it.' The Committee
looked upon one another like distracted men,
not imagining what I presently did; for I
presently pulled out of my pocket six books,
and said, 'These I own, the others are coun-
terfeits, published purposely to ruin me.'
The Committee were now more vexed than

before: not one word was spoke a good while ; at last, many of them, or the greatest number of them, were of opinion to imprison me. Some were for Newgate, others for the Gate-House; but then one Brown of Sussex, called the Presbyterian beadle, whom the Company of Stationers had bribed to be my friend, by giving him a new *Book of Martyrs;* he, I say, preached unto the Committee this doctrine, that neither Newgate or the Gate-House were prisons unto which at any time the Parliament sent their prisoners : it was most convenient for the Serjeant at Arms to take me in custody.

Mr. Strickland, who had for many years been the Parliament's Ambassador or Agent in Holland, when he saw how they inclined, spoke thus :

' I came purposely into the Committee this day to see the man who is so famous in

those parts where I have so long continued:
I assure you his name is famous all over
Europe : I come to do him justice.   A book
is produced by us, and said to be his; he
denies it; we have not proved it, yet will
commit him.   Truly this is great injustice.
It is likely he will write next year, and acquaint the whole world with our injustice;
and so well he may.   It is my opinion, first
to prove the book to be his, ere he be committed.'

Another old friend of mine, Mr. R. spoke
thus :

' You do not know the many services this
man hath done for the Parliament these many
years, or how many times, in our greatest
distresses, we applying unto him, he hath
refreshed our languishing expectations.; he
never failed us of comfort in our most unhappy distresses.   I assure you his writings

have kept up the spirits both of the soldiery, the honest people of this nation, and many of us Parliament men; and now at last, for a slip of his pen (if it were his) to be thus violent against him: I must tell you, I fear the consequence urged out of the book will prove effectually true. It is my counsel, to admonish him hereafter to be more wary, and for the present to dismiss him.'

Notwithstanding any thing that was spoken on my behalf, I was ordered to stand committed to the Serjeant at Arms. The messenger attached my person, said I was his prisoner. As he was carrying me away, he was called to bring me again. Oliver Cromwell, Lieutenant-General of the army, having never seen me, caused me to be produced again, where he stedfastly beheld me for a good space, and then I went with the messenger; but instantly a young clerk of that

Committee asks the messenger what he did with me, where's the warrant? until that is signed you cannot seize Mr. Lilly, or shall Will you have an action of false imprisonment against you? So I escaped that night, but next day obeyed the warrant. That night Oliver Cromwell went to Mr. R. my friend, and said, 'What never a man to take Lilly's cause in hand but yourself? None to take his part but you? He shall not be long there.' Hugh Peters spoke much in my behalf to the Committee; but they were resolved to lodge me in the Serjeant's custody. One Millington, a drunken member, was much my enemy; and so was Cawley and Chichester, a deformed fellow, unto whom I had done several courtesies.

First thirteen days I was a prisoner; and though every day of the Committee's sitting I had a petition to deliver, yet so many churlish Presbyterians still appeared, I could not get it accepted. The last day of the thirteen, Mr. Joseph Ash was made Chairman, unto whom my cause being related, he took my petition, and said I should be bailed in despite of them all, but desired I would procure as many friends as I could to be there. Sir Arthur Hazelrigg, and Major Salloway, a person of excellent parts, appeared for me, and many now of my old friends came in. After two whole hours arguing of my cause by Sir Arthur and Major Salloway, and other friends, the matter came to this point; I should be bailed, and a Committee nominated to examine the printer. The order of the Committee being brought afterwards to him who should be Chairman, he sent me word, do what I would, he would see all the knaves hanged, ere he would examine the printer. This is the truth of the story.

The 16th of February 165$\frac{3}{4}$, my second wife died; for whose death I shed no tears. I had five hundred pounds with her as a portion, but she and her poor relations spent me one thousand pounds. *Gloria Patri, & Filio, & Spiritui Sancto: sicut erat in principio & nunc, & semper, & in sæcula sæculorum:* for the 20th of April 1655, these enemies of mine, viz. Parliament men, were turned out of doors by Oliver Cromwell. A German doctor of physick being then in London, sent me this paper:

Strophe Alcaica: Generoso Domino Gulielmo Lillio Astrologo, de dissoluto nuper Parliamento.

Quod calculasti Sydere prævio,
Miles peregit numine conscio ;
Gentis videmus nunc Senatum
Marte togaque gravi levatum.

In the time of my imprisonment, Mr. Rushworth came to visit me, and told me, the army would do as much as I had predicted unto the Parliament.

In October 1654, I married the third wife, who is signified in my nativity by *Jupiter in Libra;* and she is so totally in her conditions, to my great comfort.

In 1655, I was indicted at Hicks's-Hall by a half-witted young woman. Three several sessions she was neglected, and the Jury cast forth her bill; but the fourth time, they found it against me: I put in bail to traverse the indictment. The cause of the indictment was, for that I had given judgment upon stolen goods, and received two shillings and six-pence.—And this was said to be contrary unto an Act in King James's time made.

This mad woman was put upon this action against me by two ministers, who had framed

for her a very ingenious speech, which she
could speak without book, as she did the
day of hearing the traverse. She produced
one woman, who told the court, a son of her's
was run from her; that being in much afflic-
tion of mind for her loss, she repaired unto
me to know what was become of him; that
I told her he was gone for the Barbadoes,
and she would hear of him within thirteen
days; which, she said, she did.

A second woman made oath, that her husband being wanting two years, she repaired
to me for advice: that I told her he was in
Ireland, and would be at home such a time;
and, said she, he did come home accordingly.

I owned the taking of half a crown for my
judgment of the theft; but said, I gave no
other judgment, but that the goods would
not be recovered, being that was all which
was required of me: the party, before that,

having been with several astrologers, some affirming she should have her goods again, others gave contrary judgment, which made her come unto me for a final resolution.

At last my enemy began her before-made speech, and, without the least stumbling, pronounced it before the court; which ended, she had some queries put unto her, and then I spoke for myself, and produced my own *Introduction* into court, saying, that I had some years before emitted that book for the benefit of this and other nations; that it was allowed by authority, and had found good acceptance in both universities; that the study of astrology was lawful, and not contradicted by any scripture; that I neither had, or ever did, use any charms, sorceries, or inchantments related in the bill of indictment, &c.

She then related, that she had been several

times with me, and that afterwards she could not rest a-nights, but was troubled with bears, lions, and tygers, &c. My counsel was the Recorder Green, who after he had answered all objections, concluded astrology was a lawful art.

' Mistress,' said he, ' what colour was those beasts that you were so terrified with?'

' I never saw any,' said she.

' How do you then know they were lions, tygers, or bears?' replied he.—' This is an idle person, only fit for Bedlam.' The Jury who went not from the bar, brought in, No true Bill.

There were many Presbyterian Justices much for her, and especially one Roberts, a busy fellow for the Parliament, who after his Majesty came in, had like to have lost life and fortune.

I had procured Justice Hooker to be there,

who was the oracle of all the Justices of Peace in Middlesex.

There was nothing memorable after that happened unto me, until 1650, and the month of October, at what time Captain Owen Cox brought me over from his Majesty of Sweden, a gold chain and medal, worth about fifty pounds; the cause whereof was, that in the year 1657 and 1658, I had made honourable mention of him: the *Anglicus* of 1658 being translated into the language spoke at Hamburgh, printed and cried about the streets, as it is in London.

The occasion of my writing so honourably of his Majesty of Sweden was this: Sir Bolstrode Whitlock, Knight, upon the very time of Oliver's being made Protector, having made very noble articles betwixt Christina then Queen of Sweden, and the English nation, was in his being at Stockholm visited

frequently by Charles Gustavus, unto whom
Christina resigned during his abode, and used
with all manner of civility by him, insomuch
as some other Ambassadors took it ill, that
they had not so much respect or equal: unto
which he would reply, he would be kind
where himself did find just cause of merit
unto any. He were a great lover of our nation; but there were some other causes also
moving my pen to be so liberal, viz. The
great hopes I had of his prevailing, and of
taking Copenhagen and Elsinore, which, if he
had lived, was hoped he might have accomplished; and had assuredly done, if Oliver
the Protector had not so untimely died ere
our fleet of ships returned; for Oliver sent
the fleet on purpose to fight the Dutch; but
dying, and the Parliament being restored,
Sir Henry Vane, who afterwards was beheaded, had order from the Council of State to

give order to the fleet what to do now Oliver was dead, and themselves restored. Vane, out of state-policy, gave the Earl of Sandwich direction not to fight the Dutch. Captain Symons, who carried those letters, swore unto me, had he known the letters he carried had contained any such prohibition, he would have sunk both ship and letters. Oliver said, when the fleet was to go forth, ' That if God blessed his Majesty of Sweden with Copenhagen, the English were to have Elsinore as their share; which if once I have,' saith Oliver, ' the English shall have the whole trade of the Baltick Sea: I will make the Dutch find another passage, except they will pay such customs as I shall impose.' Considering the advantages this would have been to our English, who can blame my pen for being liberal, thereby to have encouraged our famous and noble seamen, or for writing

so honourably of the Swedish nation, who
had most courteously treated my best of
friends, Sir Bolstrode Whitlock, and by whose
means, had the design taken effect, the English nation had been made happy with the
most beneficial concern of all Christendom.
I shall conclude about Oliver the then Protector, with whom obliquely I had transactions by his son-in-law, Mr. Cleypool; and
to speak truly of him, he sent one that waited upon him in his chamber, once in two or
three days, to hear how it fared with me in
my sessions business; but I never had of him,
directly or indirectly, either pension, or any
the least sum of money, or any gratuity during his whole Protectorship; this I protest
to be true, by the name and in the name of
the most holy God.

In 1653, before the dissolution of the Parliament, and that ere they had chosen any for

OLIVER CROMWELL.

From an original Picture by Walker

R.Cooper sculp.^t

their Ambassador into Sweden, Mr. Cleypool came unto me, demanding of me whom
I thought fittest to send upon that ambassy
into Sweden: I nominated Sir B. Whitlock,
who was chosen, and two or three days after
Mr. Cleypool came again: 'I hope, Mr. Lilly,
my father hath now pleased you: Your friend
Sir B. Whitlock is to go for Sweden.'   But
since I have mentioned Oliver Cromwell, I
will relate something of him, which perhaps
no other pen can, or will mention.   He was
born of generous parents in Huntingdonshire,
educated some time at the university of Cambridge: in his youth was wholly given to debauchery, quarrelling, drinking, &c. *quid non;*
having by those means wasted his patrimony,
he was enforced to bethink himself of leaving
England, and go to New-England: he had
hired a passage in a ship, but ere she launch-

ed out for her voyage, a kinsman dieth, leaving him a considerable fortune; upon which he returns, pays his debts, became affected to religion; is elected in 1640 a member of Parliament, in 1642 made a Captain of horse under Sir Philip Stapleton, fought at Edge-Hill; after he was made a Colonel, then Lieutenant-General to the Earl of Manchester, who was one of the three Generals to fight the Earl of Newcastle and Prince Rupert at York: Ferdinando Lord Fairfax, and Earl Leven the Scot, were the other two for the Parliament: the last two thinking all had been lost at Marston-Moor fight, Fairfax went into Cawood Castle, giving all for lost: at twelve at night there came word of the Parliament's victory; Fairfax being then laid down upon a bed, there was not a candle in the castle, nor any fire: up riseth Lord Fairfax, procures after some time, paper, ink, and candle, writes to Hull, and other garrisons of the Parliament's, of the success, and then slept.

Leven the Scot asked the way to Tweed: the honour of that day's fight was given to Manchester, Sir Thomas Fairfax's brigade of horse, and Oliver Cromwell's iron sides; for Cromwell's horse, in those times, usually wore head-pieces, back and breast-plates of iron. After this victory Cromwell became gracious with the House of Commons, especially the Zealots, or Presbyterians, with whom at that time he especially joined; the name Independent, at that time, viz. 1644, being not so much spoken of.

There was some animosity at or before the fight, betwixt the Earl of Newcastle and Prince Rupert; for Newcastle being General of his Majesty's forces in the North, a person

N

of valour, and well esteemed in those parts, took it not well to have a competitor in his concernments; for if the victory should fall on his Majesty's side, Prince Rupert's forces would attribute it unto their own General, viz. Rupert, and give him the glory thereof: but that it happened, Prince Rupert, in that day's fight, engaged the Parliament's forces too soon, and before the Earl of Newcastle could well come out of York with his army; by reason whereof, though Rupert had absolutely routed the Scots and the Lord Fairfax's forces; yet ere timely assistance could second his army, Sir Thomas Fairfax and Cromwell had put him to flight, and not long after all Newcastle's army. A most memorable action happened on that day. There was one entire regiment of foot belonging to Newcastle, called the Lambs, because they were all new cloathed in white woollen cloth, two or three days before the fight. This sole regi-

ment, after the day was lost, having got into
a small parcel of ground ditched in, and not
of easy access of horse, would take no quarter; and by mere valour, for one whole hour,
kept the troops of horse from entering
amongst them at near push of pike: when
the horse did enter, they would have no quarter, but fought it out till there was not thirty
of them living; those whose hap it was to
be beaten down upon the ground as the troopers came near them, though they could not
rise for their wounds, yet were so desperate
as to get either a pike or sword, or piece of
them, and to gore the troopers' horses as they
came over them, or passed by them. Captain
Camby, then a trooper under Cromwell, and
an actor, who was the third or fourth man
that entered amongst them, protested, he
never in all the fights he was in, met with
such resolute brave fellows, or whom he

pitied so much, and said, 'he saved two or three against their wills.'

After the fight, Manchester marched slowly southward, &c. but at last came with his army to Newbury fight; which ended, he came for London, and there he accuseth Cromwell, being his Lieutenant, to the Parliament, of disobedience, and not obeying his orders.

The House of Commons acquaint Cromwell herewith, and charge him. as he would answer it before God, that the day following he should give them a full account of Manchester's proceedings, and the cause and occasion of their difference, and of the reasons why Manchester did not timely move westward for the relief of Essex, then in the west, who was absolutely routed, inforced to fly, all his foot taken, and all his ordnance and train of artillery, only the horse escaping.

Cromwell the next day gave this account to Mr. Speaker in the House of Commons— by way of recrimination.

That after God had given them a successful victory at Marston over the King's forces, and that they had well refreshed their army, Manchester, by their order, did move southward, but with such slowness, that sometimes he would not march for three days together; sometimes he would lie still one day, then two days; whereupon he said, considering the Earl of Essex was in the west, with what success he then knew not, he moved Manchester several times to quicken his march to the west, for relief of Essex, if he were beaten, or to divert the King's forces from following of Essex; but he said Manchester still refused to make any haste; and that one day he said, ' If any man but yourself, Lieutenant, should so frequently trouble me, I would call him before a Council of War. We have beaten the King's forces in the north; if we should do so in the west, his Majesty is then undone: he hath many sons living; if any of them come to the Crown, as they well may, they will never forget us.' This Major Hammond, a man of honour, will justify as well as myself. After which he marched not at all, until he had order from the Committee to hasten westward, by reason of Essex's being lost in Cornwall, which then he did; and at Newbury fight, it is true, I refused to obey his directions and order : for this it was; his Majesty's horse being betwixt four and five thousand in a large common, in good order, he commands me, Mr. Speaker, to charge them; we having no way to come at them but through a narrow lane, where not above three horse could march abreast; whereby had I followed his order, we had been all cut off ere we could have got into any order. Mr. Speaker, (and then he wept; which he could do *toties quoties*) I, considering that all the visible army you then had, was by this counsel in danger to be lost, refused thus to endanger the main strength, which now most of all consisted of those horse under my command, &c.—This his recrimination was well accepted by the House of Commons, who thereupon, and from that time, thought there was none of the House of Lords very fit to be entrusted with their future armies, but had then thoughts of making a commoner their General; which afterwards they did, and elected Sir Thomas Fairfax their General, and Cromwell Lieutenant-General; but it was next spring first. Upon Essex's being lost in Cornwall, I heard Serjeant Maynard say, 'If now the King haste to London we are undone, having no army to resist him.'

His Majesty had many misfortunes ever attending him, during his abode at Oxford; some by reason of that great animosity betwixt Prince Rupert and the Lord Digby, each endeavouring to cross one another; but the worst of all was by treachery of several officers under his command, and in his service; for the Parliament had in continual pay one Colonel of the King's Council of War; one Lieutenant-Colonel; one Captain; one Ensign; one or two Serjeants; several Corporals, who had constant pay, and duly paid them every month, according to the capacity of their officers and places, and yet none of these knew any thing of each other's being so employed. There were several well-wishers unto the Parliament in Oxford, where each left his letter, putting it in at the hole of a glass-window, as he made water in the street What was put in at the window in any of those houses, was the same day conveyed two miles off by some in the habit of town-gardeners, to the side of a ditch, where one or more were ever ready to give the intelligence to the next Parliament garrison: I was then familiar with all the spies that constantly went in and out to Oxford.

But once more to my own actions. I had, in 1652 and 1653 and 1654, much contention with Mr. Gatacre of Rotherhithe, a man endued with all kind of learning, and the ablest man of the whole synod of divines in the Oriental tongues.

The synod had concluded to make an exposition upon the bible; some undertook one book, some another. Gatacre fell upon *Jeremy*. Upon making his exposition on the 2d verse of the 10th chapter,

' Learn not the way of the heathen, and

be not dismayed at the signs of heaven, for the heathen are dismayed at them.'

In his *Annotations* thereupon, he makes a scandalous exposition; and in express terms, hints at me, repeating *verbatim*, ten or twelve times, an *Epistle* of mine in one of my former *Anglicus.*

The substance of my *Epistle* was, that I did conceive the good angels of God did first reveal astrology unto mankind, &c. but he in his *Annotations* calls me blind buzzard, &c.

Having now liberty of the press, and hearing the old man was very cholerick, I thought fit to raise it up—and only wrote—I referred my discourse then in hand to the discussion and judgment of sober persons, but not unto Thomas Wiseacre, for *Senes bis pueri :* These very words begot the writing of forty-two sheets against myself and astrology. The next year I quibbled again in three or four lines against him, then he printed twenty-two sheets against me. I was persuaded by Dr. Gauden, late Bishop of Exeter, to let him alone; but in my next year's *Angli-cus*, in August observations, I wrote, *Hâc in tumbâ jacet Presbyter & Nebulo,* in which very month he died.

Several divines applied themselves unto me, desiring me to forbear any further vexing of Mr. Gatacre; but all of them did as much condemn him of indiscretion, that in so sober a piece of work as that was, viz. in an *Annotation* upon a sacred text of scripture to particularize me and in that dirty language: they pitied him, that he had not better considered with himself ere he published it.

Dean Owen of Christ's-Church in Oxford, also in his sermons had sharp invectives

against me and astrology ; I cried quittance
with him, by urging Abbot Panormitan's
judgment of astrology contrary to Owen's,
and concluded, 'An Abbot was an ace above
a Dean.'

One Mr. Nye of the assembly of divines,
a Jesuitical Presbyterian, bleated forth his
judgment publickly against me and astrology : to be quit with him, I urged Causinus
the Jesuit's approbation of astrology, and
concluded, *Sic canibus catulos, &c.*

In some time after the Dutch Ambassador
being offended with some things in *Anglicus*,
presented a memorial to the Council of State,
that *Merlinus Anglicus* might be considered,
and the abuses against their nation examined;
but his paper was not accepted of, or I any
way molested.

In Oliver's Protectorship, I wrote freely
and satyrical enough : he was now become

Independant, and all the soldiery my friends;
for when he was in Scotland, the day of one
of their fights, a soldier stood with *Anglicus*
in his hand; and as the several troops passed
by him, ' Lo, hear what Lilly saith; you are
in this month promised victory, fight it out,
brave boys;' and then read that month's prediction.

I had long before predicted the downfall
of Presbytery, as you (most honoured Sir)
in the figure thereof, in my *Introduction*, may
observe; and it was upon this occasion. Sir
Thomas Middleton of Chark Castle, enemy
to Presbytery, seeing they much prevailed,
being a member of the House, seriously demanded my judgment, if Presbytery should
prevail, or not, in England? The figure
printed in my *Introduction*, will best give
you an account, long before it happened, of
the sinking and failing of Presbytery; so

will the second page of my *Hieroglyphicks*.
Those men, to be serious, would preach well;
but they were more lordly than Bishops,
and usually, in their parishes, more tyrannical
than the Great Turk.

OF THE YEAR 1660; THE ACTIONS WHERE-
OF, AS THEY WERE REMARKABLE IN
ENGLAND, SO WERE THEY NO LESS ME-
MORABLE AS TO MY PARTICULAR FOR-
TUNE AND PERSON.

Upon the Lord General Monk's returning
from Scotland with his army into England,
suddenly after his coming to London, Richard
Cromwell, the then Protector's, authority was
laid aside, and the old Parliament restored;
the Council of State sat as formerly. The
first act they put the General upon was, to

take down the city gates and portcullisses, an act which, the General said, was fitter for a Janizary to do than for a General; yet he effected the commands received, and then lodged in the city with his army. The citizens took this pulling down of their gates so heinously, that one night the ruder sort of them procured all the rumps of beef, and other baggage, and publickly burnt them in the streets, in derision of the then Parliament, calling them that now sat, The Rump. This hurly-burly was managed as well by the General's soldiers as the citizens. The King's health was publickly drank all over the city, to the confusion of the Parliament. The matter continued until midnight, or longer. The Council of State, sitting at White-Hall, had hereof no knowledge, until Sir Martin Noell, a discreet citizen, came about nine at night, and then first informed them thereof.

The Council could not believe it, until they had sent some ministers of their own, who affirmed the verity thereof. They were at a stand, and could not resolve what to do; at last Nevil Smith came, being one of them, and publickly protested there was but one way to regain their authority, and to be revenged of this affront, and to overthrow the Lord General Monk, whom they now perceived intended otherways than he had pretended; his council was, to take away Monk's commission, and to give a present commission to Major-General Lambert to be their General; which counsel of his, if they would take and put it speedily in execution, would put an end unto all the present mischiefs. The Council in general did all very well approve Nevil Smith's judgment; but presently up starts Sir Arthur Hazellrigg, and makes a sharp invective against Lambert, and concluded, he would rather perish under the King of Scot's power, than that Lambert should ever any more have command under the Parliament.

The Lord General suddenly after brings in the long excluded Members to sit in Parliament, being persons of great judgment, and formerly enforced from sitting therein by the soldiery, and connivance of those who stiled themselves the godly part of the Parliament. These honourable patriots presently voted his Majesty's coming into England, and so he did in May 1660. But because Charles the Second, now (1667) King of England, Son of Charles the First, grandchild to James the First, King of Great Britany, was so miraculously restored, and so many hundreds of years since prophesied of by Ambrose Merlin, it will not be impertinent to mention the pro-

phecies themselves, the rather because we
have seen their verification.

AMBROSE MERLIN'S PROPHECY WROTE ABOUT 990 YEARS SINCE.

He calls King James, The Lion of Right-
eousness; and saith, when he died, or was
dead, there would reign a noble White King;
this was Charles the First. The prophet discovers all his troubles, his flying up and down,
his imprisonment, his death; and calls him
Aquila. What concerns Charles the Second,
is the subject of our discourse: in the Latin
copy it is thus:

*Deinde ab Austro veniet cum Sole super lig-
neos equos, & super spumantem inundationem
maris, Pullus Aquilæ navigans in Britanniam.*

*Et applicans statim tunc altam domum Aquilæ
sitiens, & cito aliam sitiet.*

Deinde Pullus Aquilæ nidificabit in summa rupe totius Britanniæ : nec juvenis occidet, nec ad senem vivet.

This, in an old copy, is Englished thus :

' After then, shall come through the south with the sun, on horse of tree, and upon all waves of the sea, the Chicken of the Eagle, sailing into Britain, and arriving anon to the house of the Eagle, he shall shew fellowship to them beasts.

' After, the Chicken of the Eagle shall nestle in the highest rock of all Britain : nay, he shall nought be slain young; nay, he nought come old.'

Another Latin copy renders the last verse thus :

Deinde pullus Aquilæ nidificabit in summo rupium, nec juvenis occidetur, nec ad senium perveniet. There is after this, *percificato regno omnes occidet ;* which is intended of those persons put to death, that sat as Judges upon his father's death.

THE VERIFICATION.

His Majesty being in the Low-Countries when the Lord General had restored the secluded Members, the Parliament sent part of the Royal Navy to bring him for England, which they did in May 1660. Holland is East from England, so he came with the sun; but he landed at Dover, a port in the south part of England. Wooden-horses, are the English ships.

Tunc nidificabit in summo rupium.

The Lord General, and most of the gentry in England, met him in Kent, and brought him unto London, then to White-hall.

Here, by the highest Rooch, (some write Rock,) is intended London, being the metropolis of all England.

Since which time, unto this very day I write this story, he hath reigned in England, and long may he do hereafter. 10th December, 1667.

Had I leisure, I might verify the whole preceding part concerning King Charles. Much of the verification thereof is mentioned in my *Collection of Prophecies*, printed 1645. But his Majesty being then alive, I forbore much of that subject, not willing to give offence. I dedicated that book unto him; and, in the conclusion thereof, I advised his return unto Parliament, with these words, *Fac hoc & vives*.

There was also a *Prophecy* printed 1588, in Greek characters, exactly decyphering the long troubles the English nation had from 1641 until 1660; and then it ended thus:

' And after that shall come a dreadful dead

man, and with him a Royal G.' [it is Gamma
in the Greek, intending C. in the Latin, being
the third letter in the alphabet,] ' of the best
blood in the world, and he shall have the
Crown, and shall set England on the right
way, and put out all heresies.'

Monkery being extinguished above eighty
or ninety years, and the Lord General's name
being Monk, is the Dead Man. The Royal
G. or C. is Charles the Second, who, for his
extraction, may be said to be of the best
blood in the world.

These two prophecies were not given vocally by the angels, but by inspection of the
crystal in types and figures, or by apparition
the circular way, where, at some distance, the
angels appear, representing by forms, shapes,
and creatures, what is demanded. It is very
rare, yea, even in our days, for any operator

or master to have the angels speak articulately; when they do speak, it is like the
Irish, much in the throat.

What further concerns his Majesty, will
more fully be evident about 1672 or 1674, or,
at farthest, in 1676.   And now unto my own
actions in 1660.

In the first place, my fee-farm rents, being
of the yearly value of one hundred and twenty
pounds, were all lost by his Majesty's coming to his restoration; but I do say truly, the
loss thereof did never trouble me, or did I re-
pine thereat.

In June of that year, a new Parliament was
called, whereunto I was unwillingly invited by two messengers of the Serjeant at Arms.
The matter whereupon I was taken into custody was, to examine me concerning the person who cut off the King's head, viz. the late
King's.

Sir Daniel Harvey, of Surry, got the business moved against me in great displeasure, because, at the election of new knights for Surrey, I procured the whole town of Walton to stand, and give their voices for Sir Richard Onslow. The Committee to examine me, were Mr. Prinn, one Colonel King, and Mr. Richard Weston of Gray's-Inn.

God's providence appeared very much for me that day, for walking in Westminster-Hall, Mr. Richard Pennington, son to my old friend Mr. William Pennington, met me, and enquiring the cause of my being there, said no more, but walked up and down the hall, and related my kindness to his father unto very many Parliament men of Cheshire and Lancashire, Yorkshire, Cumberland, and those northern countries, who numerously came up into the Speaker's chamber, and bade me be of good comfort: at last he meets Mr. Weston, one of the three unto whom my matter was referred for examination, who told Mr. Pennington, that he came purposely to punish me, and would be bitter against me; but hearing it related, viz. my singular kindness and preservation of old Mr. Pennington's estate to the value of six or seven thousand pounds, ' I will do him all the good I can,' says he. ' I thought he had never done any good; let me see him, and let him stand behind me where I sit:' I did so. At my first appearance, many of the young members affronted me highly, and demanded several scurrilous questions. Mr. Weston held a paper before his mouth; bade me answer nobody but Mr. Prinn; I obeyed his command, and saved myself much trouble thereby; and when Mr. Prinn put any difficult or doubtful query unto me, Mr. Weston prompted me with a fit answer. At last,

after almost one hour's tugging, I desired to
be fully heard what I could say as to the person who cut Charles the First's head off.
Liberty being given me to speak, I related
what follows, viz.

That the next Sunday but one after Charles
the First was beheaded, Robert Spavin, Secretary unto Lieutenant-General Cromwell
at that time, invited himself to dine with me,
and brought Anthony Peirson, and several
others, along with him to dinner: that their
principal discourse all dinner-time was only,
who it was that beheaded the King; one said
it was the common hangman; another, Hugh
Peters; others also were nominated, but none
concluded. Robert Spavin, so soon as dinner was done, took me by the hand, and carried me to the south window: saith he,
' These are all mistaken, they have not named
the man that did the fact: it was Lieutenant-

Colonel JOICE; I was in the room when he fitted himself for the work, stood behind him when he did it; when done, went in again with him: there is no man knows this but my master, viz. Cromwell, Commissary Ireton, and myself.' ' Doth not Mr. Rushworth know it?' said I. ' No, he doth not know it,' saith Spavin. The same thing Spavin since had often related unto me when we were alone. Mr. Prinn did, with much civility, make a report hereof in the House; yet Norfolk the Serjeant, after my discharge, kept me two days longer in arrest, purposely to get money of me. He had six pounds, and his Messenger forty shillings; and yet I was attached but upon Sunday, examined on Tuesday, and then discharged, though the covetous Serjeant detained me until Thursday. By means of a friend, I cried quittance with Norfolk, which friend was to pay him his salary at that time, and abated Norfolk three pounds, which we spent every penny at one dinner, without inviting the wretched Serjeant: but in the latter end of the year, when the King's Judges were arraigned at the Old-Bailey, Norfolk warned me to attend, believing I could give information concerning Hugh Peters. At the sessions I attended during its continuance, but was never called or examined. There I heard Harrison, Scott, Clement, Peters, Hacker, Scroop, and others of the King's Judges, and Cook the Sollicitor, who excellently defended himself; I say, I did hear what they could say for themselves, and after heard the sentence of condemnation pronounced against them by the incomparably modest and learned Judge Bridgman, now Lord Keeper of the Great Seal of England.

One would think my troubles for that year

had been ended; but in January 166$\frac{1}{4}$, one
Everard, a Justice of Peace in Westminster,
ere I was stirring, sent a Serjeant and thirty
four musqueteers for me to White-Hall: he
had twice that night seized about sixty persons, supposed fanaticks, very despicable
persons, many whereof were aged, some
were water-bearers, and had been Parlia-
ment-soldiers; others, of ordinary callings:
all these were guarded unto White-Hall,
into a large room, until day-light, and then
committed to the Gate-House; I was had into
the guard-room, which I thought to be hell;
some therein were sleeping, others swearing,
others smoking tobacco. In the chimney
of the room I believe there was two bushels
of broken tobacco-pipes, almost half one
load of ashes. Everard, about nine in the
morning, comes, writes my mittimus for the
Gate-House, then shews it me: I must be

contented. I desired no other courtesy, but
that I might be privately carried unto the
Gate-House by two soldiers ; that was denied. Among the miserable crew of people,
with a whole company of soldiers, I marched
to prison, and there for three hours was in
the open air upon the ground, where the
common house of office came down. After
three hours, I was advanced from this stink-
ing place up the stairs, where there was on
one side a company of rude swearing persons;
on the other side many Quakers, who lovingly entertained me. As soon as I was fixed,
I wrote to my old friend Sir Edward Walker,
Garter King at Arms, who presently went to
Mr. Secretary Nicholas, and acquainted him
with my condition. He ordered Sir Edward
to write to Everard to release me, unless he
had any particular information against me,
which he had not. He further said, it was

not his Majesty's pleasure that any of his subjects should be thus had to prison without good cause shewed before. Upon receipt of Sir Edward's letter, Everard discharged me, I taking the oaths of allegiance and supremacy. This day's work cost me thirty-seven shillings. Afterwards Everard stood to be Burgess for Westminster; sent me to procure him voices. I returned answer, that of all men living he deserved no courtesy from me, nor should have any.

In this year 1660, I sued out my pardon under the Broad Seal of England, being so advised by good counsel, because there should be no obstruction; I passed as William Lilly, Citizen and Salter of London; it cost me thirteen pounds six shillings and eight pence.

There happened a verification of an astrological judgment of mine in this year, 1660, which, because it was predicted sixteen years before it came to pass, and the year expressly nominated, I thought fit to mention.

In page 111 of my *Prophetical Merlin*, upon three sextile Aspects of Saturn and Jupiter, made in 1659 and 1660, I wrote thus—

' This their friendly salutation comforts us in England, every man now possesses his own vineyard; our young youth grow up unto man's estate, and our old men live their full years; our nobles and gentlemen root again; our yeomanry, many years disconso-lated, now take pleasure in their husbandry. The merchant sends out ships, and hath pros-perous returns; the mechanick hath quick trading: here is almost a new world; new laws, new Lords. Now my country of England shall shed no more tears, but rejoice with, and in the many blessings God gives or affords her annually.'

And in the same book, page 118, over-against the year 1660, you shall find, A bonny Scot acts his part.

The long Parliament would give Charles the Second no other title than King of Scots.

I also wrote to Sir Edward Walker, Kt. Garter King at Arms in 1659, he then being in Holland—

Tu, Dominusque vester videbitis Angliam, infra duos annos.—For in 1662, his moon came by direction to the body of the sun.

But he came in upon the ascendant directed unto the trine of Sol and antiscion of Jupiter.

And happy it was for the nation he did come in, and long and prosperously may he reign amongst us.

P

In 1663 and 1664, I had a long and tedious law-suit in Chancery, M. C. coming to quartile of Saturn; and the occasion of that suit, was concerning houses; and my enemy, though aged, had no beard, was really saturnine. We came unto a hearing Feb. 166¾, before the Master of the Rolls, Sir Harbottle Grimston, where I had the victory, but no costs given me.

My adversary, not satisfied with that judgment, petitioned that most just and honourable man, the Lord Chancellor Hyde, for a re-hearing his cause before him.

It was granted, and the 13th June, 1664, my M. C. then directed to quartile of Venus and Sol. His Lordship most judiciously heard it with much attention, and when my adversary's counsel had urged those depositions which they had against me, his Lordship stood up, and said,

' Here is not one word against Mr. Lilly.'—

I replied, ' My Lord, I hope I shall have costs.'

' Very good reason,' saith he; and so I had : and, at my departure out of court, put off his hat, and bid ' God be with you.'

This is the month of Dec. 1667, wherein, by misfortune, he is much traduced and high-ly persecuted by his enemies : is also retired, however not in the least questioned for any indirect judgment as Chancellor, in the Chan-cery ; [but in other things he hath been very foul, as in the articles drawn up by the Par-liament against him, it appears.   Which arti-cles I presume you have not seen, otherwise you would have been of another mind, A W] for there was never any person sat in that place, who executed justice with more up-rightness, or judgment, or quickness for dis-patch, than this very noble Lord.   God, I hope, in mercy will preserve his person from his enemies, and in good time restore him unto all his honours again: from my soul I wish it, and hope I shall live to see it. Amen: *Fiat oh tu Deus justitiæ.*

In 1663 and 1664, I was made church-warden of Walton upon Thames, settling as well as I could the affairs of that distracted parish, upon my own charges; and upon my leaving the place, forgave them seven pounds odd money due unto me.

In 1664, I had another law-suit with Captain Colborn, Lord of the manor of Esher, concerning the rights of the parish of Walton. He had newly purchased that manor, and having one hundred and fifty acres of ground, formerly park and wood ground lying in our parish, conceived, he had right of common in our parish of Walton: thereupon he puts three hundred sheep upon the common; part whereof I impounded: he replevins them, and gave me a declaration. I answered it. The trial was to be at the Assizes at Kingston in April 1664. When the day of trial came, he had not one witness in his cause, I had many; whereupon upon conference, and by mediation, he gave me eleven pounds for my charges sustained in that suit, whereof I returned him back again fifty shillings: forty shillings for himself, and ten shillings for the poor of the parish he lived in.

This I did at my own cost and charges, not one parishioner joining with me. I had now M. C. under quartile of Venus and Sol —both in my second, ergo, I got money by this thing, or suit. Sir Bolstrode Whitlock gave me counsel.

Now I come unto the year 1665, wherein that horrible and devouring plague so extreamly raged in the city of London. 27th

of June 1665, I retired into the country to
my wife and family, where since I have
wholly continued, and so intend by permis-
sion of God. I had, before I came away,
very many people of the poorer sort frequented my lodging, many whereof were so
civil, as when they brought waters, viz.
urines, from infected people, they would
stand purposely at a distance. I ordered
those infected, and not like to die, cordials,
and caused them to sweat, whereby many
recovered. My landlord of the house was
afraid of those poor people, I nothing at all.
He was desirous I should be gone. He had
four children: I took them with me into the
country and provided for them. Six weeks
after I departed, he, his wife, and man-servant
died of the plague.

In *Monarchy or no Monarchy*, printed 1651,
I had framed an Hieroglyphick, which you

may see in page the 7th, representing a great sickness and mortality; wherein you may see the representation of people in their winding-sheets, persons digging graves and sepultures, coffins, &c. All this was performed by the more secret *Key of Astrology*, or *Prophetical Astrology*.

In 1666, happened that miraculous conflagration in the city of London, whereby in four days, the most part thereof was consumed by fire. In my *Monarchy or no Monarchy*, the next side after the coffins and pickaxes, there is a representation of a great city all in flames of fire. The memorial whereof some Parliament men remembering, thought fit to send for me before that Committee which then did sit, for examination of the causes of the fire; and whether there was no treachery or design in the business, his Majesty being then in war both with the French and Dutch.

The summons to appear before that Committee was as followeth.

"*Monday,* 22*d October,* 1666.

"At the Committee appointed to enquire after the causes of the late fires:

"ORDERED,

"That Mr. Lilly do attend this Committee on Friday next, being the 25th of October, 1666, at two of the clock in the afternoon, in the Speaker's chamber; to answer such questions as shall be then and there asked him.

"ROBERT BROOKE."

By accident I was then in London, when the summons came unto me. I was timorous of Committees, being ever by some of them calumniated, upbraided, scorned, and derided. However I must and did appear; and

let me never forget that great affection and
care yourself (Oh most excellent and learned
Esquire Ashmole) shewed unto me at that
time. First, your affection in going along
with me all that day; secondly, your great
pains and care, in speaking unto many worthy Members of that Committee your acquaintance, that they should befriend me,
and not permit me to be affronted, or have
any disgraceful language cast upon me. I
must seriously acknowledge the persuasions
so prevailed with those generous souls, that
I conceive there was never more civility used
unto any than unto myself; and you know,
there were no small number of Parliament
men appeared, when they heard I was to be
there.

Sir Robert Brooke spoke to this purpose:
' Mr. Lilly, This Committee thought fit to
summon you to appear before them this day,

to know, if you can say any thing as to the cause of the late fire, or whether there might be any design therein. You are called the rather hither, because in a book of your's, long since printed, you hinted some such thing by one of your hieroglyphics.' Unto which I replied,

'May it please your Honours,

'After the beheading of the late King, considering that in the three subsequent years the Parliament acted nothing which concerned the settlement of the nation in peace; and seeing the generality of people dissatisfied, the citizens of London discontented, the soldiery prone to mutiny, I was desirous, according to the best knowledge God had given me, to make enquiry by the art I studied, what might from that time happen unto the Parliament and nation in general. At last, having

satisfied myself as well as I could, and perfected my judgment therein, I thought it most
convenient to signify my intentions and conceptions thereof, in Forms, Shapes, Types,
Hieroglyphicks, &c. without any commentary, that so my judgment might be concealed
from the vulgar, and made manifest only unto
the wise.   I herein imitating the examples of
many wise philosophers who had done the
like.'

' Sir Robert,' saith one, ' Lilly is yet *sub
vestibulo*.'

I proceeded further.   Said I, ' Having
found, Sir, that the city of London should be
sadly afflicted with a great plague, and not
long after with an exorbitant fire, I framed
these two hieroglyphics as represented in the
book, which in effect have proved very
true.'

' Did you foresee the year ?' said one.

'I did not,' said I, 'or was desirous: of that I made no scrutiny.' I proceeded—

'Now, Sir, whether there was any design of burning the city, or any employed to that purpose, I must deal ingenuously with you, that since the fire, I have taken much pains in the search thereof, but cannot or could not give myself any the least satisfaction therein. I conclude, that it was the only finger of God ; but what instruments he used thereunto, I am ignorant.'

The Committee seemed well pleased with what I spoke, and dismissed me with great civility.

Since which time no memorable action hath happened unto me, my retirement im peding all concourse unto me.

I have many things more to communicate, which I shall do, as they offer themselves to memory.

In anno 1634, and 1635, I had much familiarity with John Hegenius, Doctor of Physick, a Dutchman, an excellent scholar and an able physician, not meanly versed in astrology. Unto him, for his great civility, I communicated the art of framing Sigils, Lamens, &c. and the use of the Mosaical Rods :—and we did create several Sigils to very good purpose. I gave him the true key thereof, *viz.* instructed him of their forms, characters, words, and last of all, how to give them vivification, and what number or numbers were appropriated to every planet : *Cum multis aliis in libris veterum latentibus ; aut perspicuè non intellectis.*

I was well acquainted with the Speculator of John a Windor, a scrivener, sometimes living in Newbury. This Windor was club-fisted, wrote with a pen betwixt both his hands. I have seen many bonds and bills wrote by him. He was much given to debauchery, so that at some times the Dæmons would not appear to the Speculator; he would then suffumigate: sometimes, to vex the spirits, he would curse them, fumigate with contraries. Upon his examination before Sir Henry Wallop, Kt. which I have seen, he said, he once visited Dr. Dee in Mortlack; and out of a book that lay in the window, he copied out that call which he used, when he invocated——

It was that—which near the beginning of it hath these words,

Per virtutem illorum qui invocant nomen tuum,
Hermeli—*mitte nobis tres Angelos, &c.*

Windor had many good parts, but was a most lewd person: My master Wright knew him well, and having dealing in those parts, made use of him as a scrivener.

R.Cooper sculp.^t

Dr JOHN DEE.

From an Original Picture in the Ashmolean Museum, Oxford.

PUBLISHED BY CHARLES & HENRY BALDWIN NEWGATE STREET

Oliver Withers, servant to Sir H. Wallop, brought up John a Windor's examination unto London, purposely for me to peruse. This Withers was Mr. Fiske's scholar three years more or less, to learn astrology of him; but being never the wiser, Fiske brought him unto me : by shewing him but how to judge one figure, his eyes were opened : He made the Epistle before Dr. Neve's book, now in Mr. Sander's hands, was very learned in the Latin, Greek, and Hebrew tongues.

Having mentioned Dr. John Dee, I hold it not impertinent to speak something of him; but more especially of Edward Kelly's Speculator.

Dr. Dee himself was a Cambro Briton, educated in the university of Oxford, there took his degree of Doctor; afterwards for many years in search of the profounder studies, travelled into foreign parts : to be serious, he was Queen Elizabeth's intelligencer, and had a salary for his maintenance from the Secretaries of State. He was a ready witted man, quick of apprehension, very learned, and of great judgment in the Latin and Greek tongues. He was a very great investigator of the more secret Hermetical learning, a perfect astronomer, a curious astrologer, a serious geometrician; to speak truth, he was excellent in all kinds of learning.

With all this, he was the most ambitious person living, and most desirous of fame and renown, and was never so well pleased as when he heard himself stiled Most Excellent.

He was studious in chymistry, and attained to good perfection therein; but his servant, or rather companion, Kelly, out-went him, *viz.* about the Elixir or Philosopher's Stone; which neither Kelly or Dee attained by their own labour and industry. It was in this manner Kelly obtained it, as I had it related from an ancient minister, who knew the certainty thereof from an old English merchant, resident in Germany, at what time both Kelly and Dee were there.

Dee and Kelly being in the confines of the Emperor's dominions, in a city where resided many English merchants, with whom they had much familiarity, there happened an old Friar to come to Dr. Dee's lodging. Knocking at the door, Dee peeped down the stairs. 'Kelly,' says he, 'tell the old man I am not at home.' Kelly did so. The Friar said, 'I will take another time to wait on him.' Some few days after, he came again. Dee ordered Kelly, if it were the same person, to deny him again. He did so; at which the Friar was very angry. 'Tell thy master I came to speak with him and to do him

good, because he is a great scholar and famous; but now tell him, he put forth a book,
and dedicated it to the Emperor: it is called
Monas Hierogliphicas. He understands it
not. I wrote it myself, I came to instruct
him therein, and in some other more profound things. Do thou, Kelly, come along
with me, I will make thee more famous than
thy master Dee.'

Kelly was very apprehensive of what the
Friar delivered, and thereupon suddenly retired from Dee, and wholly applied unto the
Friar; and of him either had the Elixir ready
made, or the perfect method of its prepara-
tion and making. The poor Friar lived a
very short time after: whether he died a
natural death, or was otherwise poisoned or
made away by Kelly, the merchant, who related this, did not certainly know.

How Kelly died afterwards at Prague, you

R.Cooper sculp.

EDWARD KELLY.

From a Print prefixed to Dr. Dee's Book of Spirits 1659.

PUBLISHED BY CHARLES & HENRY BALDWYN, NEWGATE STREET.

well know : he was born at Worcester, had
been an apothecary.   Not above thirty years
since he had a sister lived in Worcester, who
had some gold made by her brother's projec-
tion.

Dr. Dee died at Mortlack in Surrey, very
poor, enforced many times to sell some book
or other to buy his dinner with, as Dr. Napier of Linford, in Buckinghamshire, oft related, who knew him very well.

I have read over his book of *Conference
with Spirits*, and thereby perceive many
weaknesses in the manage of that way of
Mosaical learning : but I conceive, the reason why he had not more plain resolutions,
and more to the purpose, was, because Kelly
was very vicious, unto whom the angels were
not obedient, or willingly did declare the
questions propounded ; but I could give other
reasons, but those are not for paper.

I was very familiar with one Sarah Skelhorn, who had been Speculatrix unto one
Arthur Gauntlet about Gray's-Inn-Lane, a
very lewd fellow, professing physick. This
Sarah had a perfect sight, and indeed the
best eyes for that purpose I ever yet did see.
Gauntlet's books, after he was dead, were
sold, after I had perused them, to my scholar
Humphreys: there were rare notions in them.
This Sarah lived a long time, even until her
death, with one Mrs. Stockman in the Isle
of Purbeck, and died about sixteen years
since. Her mistress one time being desirous
to accompany her mother, the Lady Becons-
field, unto London, who lived twelve miles
from her habitation, caused Sarah to inspect
her crystal, to see if she, viz. her mother,
was gone, yea or not: the angels appeared,
and shewed her mother opening a trunk, and
taking out a red waistcoat, whereby she per-

ceived she wàs not gone. Next day she went to her mother's, and there, as she entered the chamber, she was opening a trunk, and had a red waistcoat in her hand. Sarah told me oft, the angels would for some years follow her, and appear in every room of the house, until she was weary of them.

This Sarah Skelhorn, her call unto the crystal began,

' *Oh ye good angels, only and only,*' &c.

Ellen Evans, daughter of my tutor Evans, her call unto the crystal was this :

' *O Micol, O tu Micol, regina pigmeorum veni, &c.*'

Since I have related of the Queen of Fairies, I shall acquaint you, that it is not for every one, or every person, that these angelical creatures will appear unto, though they may say over the call, over and over, or indeed is it given to very many persons to

endure their glorious aspects; even very
many have failed just at that present when
they are ready to manifest themselves; even
persons otherwise of undaunted spirits and
firm resolution, are herewith astonished, and
tremble; as it happened not many years
since with us. A very sober discreet person,
of virtuous life and conversation, was beyond
measure desirous to see something in this
nature. He went with a friend into my
Hurst Wood: the Queen of Fairies was invocated, a gentle murmuring wind came
first; after that, amongst the hedges, a smart
whirlwind; by and by a strong blast of wind
blew upon the face of the friend,—and the
Queen appearing in a most illustrious glory,
' No more, I beseech you,' (quoth the friend :)
' My heart fails; I am not able to endure
longer.' Nor was he : his black curling
hair rose up, and I believe a bullrush would

have beat him to the ground : he was soundly laughed at, &c.

Sir Robert Holborn, Knight, brought once unto me *Gladwell of Suffolk, who had formerly had sight and conference with Uriel and Raphael, but lost them both by carelessness; so that neither of them both would but rarely appear, and then presently be gone, resolving nothing. He would have given me two hundred pounds to have assisted him for their recovery, but I am no such man.— Those glorious creatures, if well commanded, and well observed, do teach the master any thing he desires; *Amant secreta, fugiunt aperta.* The Fairies love the southern side

---

* Mr. Gilbert Wakering gave him his berril when he died ; it was of the largeness of a good big orange, set in silver, with a cross on the top, and another on the handle ; and round about engraved the names of these angels, Raphael, Gabriel, Uriel.

of hills, mountains, groves.—Neatness and cleanliness in apparel, a strict diet, and upright life, fervent prayers unto God, conduce much to the assistance of those who are curious these ways.

It hath been my happiness to meet with many rarities in my time unexpectedly. I had a sister lived in the Minories, in that very house where formerly had lived one Evans, not my tutor, but another far exceeding him in astrology, and all other occult learning, questioned for his life about 1612. I am sure it was when the present Earl of Manchester's father was Lord Chief Justice of England. He was found guilty by a peevish Jury: but petitioning King James by a Greek petition, as indeed he was an excellent Grecian; 'By my saul,' said King James, 'this man shall not die; I think he is a better Grecian than any of my Bishops:' so his life was spared,

&c. My sister's master when new model-
ling the house, broke up a window, under
which were Evans's secret manuscripts,* and
two moulds in brass; one of a man, the other
of a woman. I bought the moulds and
book for five shillings; the secrets were
wrote in an imperfect Greek character; but
after I found the vowels, all the rest were
presently clear enough.

You see, most worthy Sir, I write freely;
it is out of the sincerity of my affection, many
things wrote by me having been more fit for a
sepulture than a book: But,

*Quo major est virorum præstantium, tui si-
milium inopia; eo mihi charior est, & esse debet
& amicitia tua: quam quidem omnibus officiis,
& studiis, quæ a summa benevolentia possunt,
perpetuò colam:* However, who study the

---

* From these manuscripts he gained his first knowledge.

curiosities before-named, if they are not very well versed in astrology, they shall rarely attain their desired ends. There was, in the late times of troubles, one Mortlack, who pretended unto Speculations, had a crystal, a call of Queen Mab, one of the Queen of Fairies; he deluded many thereby: at last I was brought into his company; he was desired to make invocation, he did so; nothing appeared, or would : three or four times in my company he was put upon to do the work, but could not; at last he said he could do nothing as long as I was in presence. I at last shewed him his error, but left him as I found him, a pretending ignoramus.

I may seem to some to write incredibilia; be it so, but knowing unto whom, and for whose only sake, I do write them, I am much comforted therewith, well knowing you are the most knowing man in these curiosities of any now living in England; and therefore it is my hope, these will be a present well-becoming you to accept.

Præclara omnia quam difficilia sint, his præsertim temporibus. (Celeberrimè Armiger,) *non te fugit;* and therefore I will acquaint you with one memorable story related unto me by Mr. John Marr, an excellent mathematican and geometrician, whom I conceive you remember: he was servant to King James and Charles the First.

At first, when the Lord Napier, or Marchiston, made publick his Logarithms, Mr. Briggs, then reader of the astronomy lecture at Gresham-College in London, was so surprized with admiration of them, that he could have no quietness in himself, until he had seen that noble person the Lord Marchiston, whose only invention they were: he acquaints John Marr herewith, who went into

Scotland before Mr. Briggs, purposely to be there when these two so learned persons should meet. Mr. Briggs appoints a certain day when to meet at Edinburgh : but failing thereof, the Lord Napier was doubtful he would not come. It happened one day as John Marr and the Lord Napier were speaking of Mr. Briggs ; ' Ah, John,' saith Marchiston, ' Mr. Briggs will not now come:' at the very instant one knocks at the gate ; John Marr hasted down, and it proved Mr. Briggs, to his great contentment. He brings Mr. Briggs up into my Lord's chamber, where almost one quarter of an hour was spent, each beholding the other almost with admiration, before one word was spoke : at last Mr. Briggs began.

'My Lord, I have undertaken this long journey purposely to see your person, and to know by what engine of wit or ingenuity

R.Cooper sculp?

NAPIER of MERCHISTON.

From a rare Print by Delaram.

PUBLISHED BY CHARLES HENRY BALDWYN, NEWGATE STREET.

you came first to think of this most excellent help unto astronomy, viz. the Logarithms; but, my Lord, being by you found out, I wonder no body else found it out before, when, now known, it is so easy.' He was nobly entertained by the Lord Napier, and every summer after that, during the Lord's being alive, this venerable man, Mr. Briggs, went purposely into Scotland to visit him; *Tempora nunc mutantur.*

These two persons were worthy men in their time; and yet the one, viz. Lord Marchiston, was a great lover of astrology, but Briggs the most satirical man against it that hath been known: but the reason hereof I conceive was, that Briggs was a severe Presbyterian, and wholly conversant with persons of that judgment; whereas the Lord Marchiston was a general scholar, and deeply read in all divine and human histories: it is

the same Marchiston who made that most
serious and learned exposition upon the *Re-*
velation of St. John; which is the best that
ever yet appeared in the world.

Thus far proceeded Mr. William Lilly in
setting down the account of his life, with
some other things of note.   Now shall be
added something more which afterwards happened during his retirement at his house at
Hersham, until his death.

He left London in the year 1665, (as he
hath before noted) and betook himself to the
study of physick; in which, having arrived
at a competent degree of knowledge, assisted
by diligent observation and practice, he desired his old friend, Mr. Ashmole, to obtain
of his Grace Dr. Sheldon, then Lord Arch-
bishop of Canterbury, a license for the practice of physick; which upon application to

his Grace, and producing a testimonial [October. 8, 1670,] under the hands of two physicians of the college in London, on Mr. Lilly's behalf, he most readily granted, in the manner following, viz.

'GILBERTUS providentia divina Cantuariensis Archiepiscopus totius Angliæ Primas & Metropolitanus, dilecto nobis in Christo GULIELMO LILLY in Medicinis Professori, salutem, gratiam, & benedictionem. Cum ex fide digna relatione acceperimus Te in arte sive facultate Medicinæ per non modicum tempus versatum fuisse, multisque de salute & sanitate corporis vere desperatis (Deo Omnipotente adjuvante) subvenisse, eosque sanasse, nec non in arte predicta multorum peritorum laudabili testimonio pro experientia, fidelitate, diligentia & industria tuis circa curas quas susceperis peragendas in hujusmodi Arte Medicinæ merito com-

mendatum esse, ad practicandum igitur &
exercendum dictam Artem Medicinæ in, &
per totam Provinciam nostram Cant' (Civi-
tate Lond' & circuitu septem milliarum eidem
prox' adjacen' tantummodo exceptis) ex
causis prædictis & aliis nos in hac per te
justè moventibus, præstito primitus per te
juramento de agnoscendo Regiam suprema
potestatem in causis ecclesiasticis & tempo-
ralibus ac de renunciando, refutando, & recu-
sando omni, & omnimodæ jurisdictioni, potes-
tati, authoritati & superioritati foraneis juxta
vim formam & effectum statui Parliamenti
hujus inclyti Regni Angliæ in ea parte editi
& provisi quantum nobis per statuta hujus
Regni Angliæ liceat & non aliter neque alio
modo te admittimus & approbamus, tibique
Licentiam & Facultatem nostras in hâc parte,
tenore præsentium quamdiu te benè & lauda-
biliter gesseris benignè concedimus & elargi-

mur.   In cujus rei testimonium sigillum (quo
in hâc parte utimur) præsentibus apponi fe-
cimus.   Dat. undecimo die mensis Octobris.
Anno Domini 1670.   Nostræque translationis
Anno Octavo.

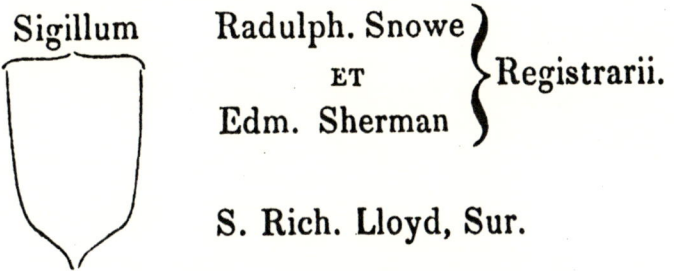

Sigillum   Radulph. Snowe ⎱
                        ET   ⎰ Registrarii.
                Edm. Sherman

                S. Rich. Lloyd, Sur.

' Vicarii in Spiritualibus Generalis
  per Provinciam Cantuariensem.'

Hereupon he began to practise more openly, and with good success; and every Saturday rode to Kingston, where the poorer sort
flocked to him from several parts, and received much benefit by his advice and pre-
scriptions, which he gave them freely, and

R

without money.   From those that were more
able, he now and then received a shilling,
and sometimes an half crown, if they offered it
to him, otherwise he demanded nothing ;
and, in truth, his charity towards poor people was very great, no less than the care and
pains he took in considering and weighing
their particular cases, and applying proper
remedies to their infirmities, which gained
him extraordinary credit and estimation.

He was of a strong constitution, and continued generally in good health, till the 16th
of August 1674, when a violent humour discovered itself in red spots all over his body,
with little pushes in his head.   This, in the
winter [18 December] following, was se-
conded by a distemper whereof he fell sick,
and was let blood in the left foot, a little
above the ancle.

The 20th of December following, a hu-

mour descended from his head to his left
side, from eight o'clock at night till the next
morning; and then staying a while in the
calf of his leg, at length descended towards
his toes, the anguish whereof put him into a
fever. This humour fixed in two places on
the top of his left foot (one in that where he
was let blood two days before) which (upon
application of pledgets) growing ripe, they
were [28 Dec.] lanced by Mr. Agar of Kingston, his apothecary (and no less a skilful
Surgeon:) after which he began to be at
ease, his fever abated, and within five months
the cure was perfected.

The 7th of November 1675, he was taken
with a violent fit of vomiting for some hours,
to which a fever succeeded, that continued
four months : this brought his body exceeding low, together with a dimness in his eyes,

which after occasioned him to make use of
Mr. Henry Coley, as his amanuensis, to transcribe (from his dictates) his astrological
judgments for the year 1677; but the month-
ly observations for that year, were written
with his own hand some time before, though
by this time he was grown very dim-sighted.
His judgments and observations for the succeeding years, till his death, (so also for the
year 1682,) were all composed by his directions, Mr. Coley coming to Hersham the beginning of every summer, and stayed there,
till, by conference with him, he had dis-
patched them for the press; to whom, at
these opportunities, he communicated his
way of judgment, and other astrological ar-
canas.

In the beginning of the year 1681, he had
a flux, which weakened him much, yet after

some time his strength encreased; but now his sight was wholly taken from him, not having any glimmering as formerly.

He had dwelt many years at Hersham, where his charity and kindness to his poor neighbours was always great and hearty; and the 30th of May 1681, towards the evening, a dead palsy began to seize his left side. The second of June, towards evening, he took his bed, and then his tongue began to falter. The next day he became very dull and heavy: sometimes his senses began to fail him. Henceforward he took little or nothing, for his larinx swelled, and that impeded his swallowing.

The fourth of June, Mr. Ashmole went to visit him, and found he knew him, but spake little, and some of that scarce intelligible; for the palsy began now to seize upon his tongue.

The eighth of June he lay in a great agony, insomuch that the sweat followed drop after drop, which he bore with wonderful courage and patience (as indeed he did all his sickness) without complaint; and about three o'clock the next morning, he died, without any shew of trouble or pangs. Immediately before his breath went from him, he sneezed three times.

He had often, in his life-time, desired Mr. Ashmole to take care of his funeral, and now his widow desired the same: whereupon Mr. Ashmole obtained leave from Sir Mathew Andrews (who had the parsonage of Walton) to bury him in the chancel of that church.

The 10th of June, his corse was brought thither, and received by the minister (in his surplice) at the Litch Gates, who, passing before the body into the church, read the first part of the *Office for the Burial of the*

Dead. In the reading desk he said all the evening service, and after performed the rest of the office (as established by law) in the chancel, at the interment, which was about eight o'clock in the evening, on the left side of the communion table, Mr. Ashmole assisting at the laying him in his grave; whereupon afterwards [9 July 1681] he placed a fair black marble stone, (which cost him six pounds four shillings and six-pence) with this inscription following:

Ne Oblivione conteretur Urna

GULIELMI LILLII

ASTROLOGI PERITISSIMI,

QUI FATIS CESSIT

Quinto Idus Junii Anno Christi Juliano

M DC LXXXI.

Hoc Illi posuit amoris Monumentum

ELIAS ASHMOLE,

ARMIGER.

Shortly after his death, Mr. Ashmole bought his library of books of Mrs. Ruth Lilly, (his widow and executrix) for fifty pounds: he oft times, in his life-time, expressed, that if Mr. Ashmole would give that sum, he should have them.

The following Epitaphs (Latin and English) were made by George Smalridge, then a scholar at Westminster, after Student of Christ-Church in Oxford.

In Mortem Viri Doctissimi Domini GULIELMI
LILLY, *Astrologi, nuper defuncti.*

Occidit atque suis annalibus addidit atram
   Astrologus, quâ non tristior ulla, diem
Pone triumphales, lugubris Luna, quadrigas ;
   Sol mæstum piceâ nube reconde caput.
Illum, qui Phœbi scripsit, Phœbesq; labores
   Eclipsin docuit Stella maligna pati.

Invidia Astrorum cecidit, qui Sidera rexit

    Tanta erat in notas scandere cura domos.

Quod vidit, visum cupiit, potiturq; cupito

    Cœlo, & Sidereo fulget in orbe decus.

Scilicet hoc nobis prædixit ab ane Cometa,

    Et fati emicuit nuncia Stella tui

Fallentem vidi faciem gemuiq; videndo

    Illa fuit vati mortis imago suo,

Civilis timuere alii primordia belli

    Jejunam metuit plebs stupefata famem

Non tantos tulerat bellumve famesve dolores :

    Auspiciis essent hæc relevanda tuis.

In cautam subitus plebem nunc opprimat ensis,

    Securos fati mors violenta trahat.

Nemo est qui videat moneatq; avertere fatum,

    Ars jacet in Domini funera mersa sui

Solus naturæ reservare arcana solebat,

    Solus & ambĭgui solvere jura poti.

Lustrâsti erantes benè finâ mente Planeta

    Conspectum latuit stellata nulla tuum

Defessos oculos pensârunt lumina mentis

    Firesias oculis, mentibus Argus eras.

Cernere, Firesia, poteras ventura, sed, Arge,

    In fatum haud poteras sat vigil esse tuum

Sed vivit nomen semper cum sole vigebit,

    Immemor Astrologi non erit ulla dies

Sæcla canent laudes, quas si percurrere cones,

    Arte opus est, Stellas quâ numerare soles

Hæreat hoc carmen cinerum custodibus urnis,

    Hospes quod spargens marmora rore legat.

" Hic situs est, dignus nunquam cecidisse Propheta;

    Fatorum interpres fata inopina subit.

Versari æthereo dum vixit in orbe solebat:

    Nunc humilem jactat Terra superba virum.

Sed Cœlum metitur adhuc resupinus in urnâ

    Vertitur in solitos palpebra clausa polos.

Huic busto invigilant solenni lampade Musæ,

    Perpetuo nubes imbre sepulchra rigant.

Ille oculis movit distantia Sidera nostris,

    Illam amota oculis traxit ad astra Deus."

An ELEGY upon the Death of WILLIAM LILLY, the Astrologer.

OUR Prophet's gone; no longer may our ears

Be charm'd with musick of th' harmonious spheres.

Let sun and moon withdraw, leave gloomy night
To shew their NUNCIO's fate, who gave more light
To th' erring world, than all the feeble rays
Of sun or moon; taught us to know those days
Bright TITAN makes; follow'd the hasty sun
Through all his circuits ; knew th' unconstant moon,
And more unconstant ebbings of the flood ;
And what is most uncertain, th' factious brood,
Flowing in civil broils : by the heavens could date
The flux and reflux of our dubious state.
He saw the eclipse of sun, and change of moon
He saw, but seeing would not shun his own:
Eclips'd he was, that he might shine more bright,
And only chang'd to give a fuller light.
He having view'd the sky, and glorious train
Of gilded stars, scorn'd longer to remain
In earthly prisons : could he a village love,
Whom the twelve houses waited for above?
The grateful stars a heavenly mansion gave
T' his heavenly soul, nor could he live a slave
To mortal passions, whose immortal mind,
Whilst here on earth, was not to earth confin'd.

He must be gone, the stars had so decreed ;
As he of them, so they of him, had need.
This message 'twas the blazing comet brought;
I saw the pale-fac'd star, and seeing thought
(For we could guess, but only LILLY knew)
It did some glorious hero's fall foreshew :
A hero's fall'n, whose death, more than a war,
Or fire, deserv'd a comet : th' obsequious star
Could do no less than his sad fate unfold,
Who had their risings, and their settings told.
Some thought a plague, and some a famine near ;
Some wars from France, some fires at home did fear :
Nor did they fear too much : scarce kinder fate,
But plague of plagues befell th' unhappy state
When LILLY died.   Now swords may safely come
From France or Rome, fanaticks plot at home.
Now an unseen, and unexpected hand,
By guidance of ill stars, may hurt our land ;
Unsafe, because secure, there's none to show
How England may avert the fatal blow.
He's dead, whose death the weeping clouds deplore,
I wish we did not owe to him that show'r

Which long expected was, and might have still
Expected been, had not our nation's ill
Drawn from the heavens a sympathetic tear :
England hath cause a second drought to fear.
We have no second LILLY, who may die,
And by his death may make the heavens cry.
Then let your annals, COLEY, want this day,
Think every year leap-year ; or if 't must stay,
Cloath it in black ; let a sad note stand by,
And stigmatize it to posterity.

*Here follows the Copy of an Indictment filed
against Mr. Lilly, for which see page* 167
of his Life.

THE jurors for the Lord Protector of the common wealth of England, Scotland, and Ireland, &c. upon their oaths do present, that William Lilly, late of the Parish of St. Clements Danes, in the County of Middlesex, Gent. not having the fear of God before his eyes, but being moved and seduced by the insti-

gation of the devil, the 10th day of July, in
the Year of our Lord, 1654, at the Parish
aforesaid, in the County aforesaid, wickedly,
unlawfully, and deceitfully, did take upon
him, the said William Lilly, by inchantment,
charm, and sorcery, to tell and declare to one
Anne East, the wife of Alexander East, where
ten waistcoats, of the value of five pounds,
of the goods and chattels of the said Alexander East, then lately before lost and stolen
from the said Alexander East, should be
found and become; and two shilling and six-
pence in monies numbred, of the monies of
the said Alexander, from the said Anne East,
then and there unlawfully and deceitfully,
he, the said William Lilly, did take, receive,
and had, to tell and declare to her the said
Anne, where the said goods, so lost and stolen
as aforesaid, should be found and become:
And also that he, the said William Lilly, on

the said tenth day of July, in the Year of our Lord, 1654, and divers other days and times, as well before as afterwards, at the said Parish aforesaid, in the County aforesaid, unlawfully and deceitfully did take upon him, the said William Lilly, by inchantment, charm, and sorcery, to tell and declare to divers other persons, to the said jurors, yet unknown, where divers goods, chattels, and things of the said persons yet unknown, there lately before lost and stolen from the said persons yet unknown, should be found and become; and divers sums of monies of the said persons yet unknown, then and there unlawfully and deceitfully, he the said William Lilly did take, receive, and had, to tell and declare to the said persons yet unknown, where their goods, chattels, and things, so lost and stolen, as aforesaid, should be found and become, in contempt of the laws of England, to the great damage and deceit of the said Alexander and Anne, and of the said other persons yet unknown, to the evil and pernicious example of all others in the like case offending, against the form of the statute in this case made and provided, and against the publick peace, &c.

> *Anne East,*
> *Emme Spencer,*
> *Jane Gold,*
> *Katherine Roberts,*
> *Susannah Hulinge.*

Butler's Character of WILLIAM LILLY.

————

*　*　*　*　*　*

* " A cunning man, hight SIDROPHEL.
That deals in destiny's dark counsels,
And sage opinions of the moon sells;
To whom all people, far and near,
On deep importances repair;
When brass and pewter hap to stray,
And linen slinks out of the way :

* *A cunning man, hight* SIDROPHEL.] " William Lilly, the famous
astrologer of those times, who in his yearly almanacks foretold victories for
the parliament with as much certainty as the Preachers did in their sermons;
and all or most part of what is ascribed to him by the Poet, the reader will
find verified in his " Letter," (if we may believe it) wrote by himself to
Elias Ashmole, Esq." For further curious information respecting William
Lilly, the reader may consult *Dr. Grey's Notes to Hudibras,* vol. ii. page
163, &c. Edition 1819, in 3 vols. 8vo.

When geese and pullen are seduc'd,
And sows of sucking pigs are chous'd :
When cattle feel indisposition,
And need th' opinion of physician;
When murrain reigns in hogs or sheep,
And chickens languish of the pip;
When yeast and outward means do fail,
And have no power to work on ale :
When butter does refuse to come,
And love proves cross and humoursome ;
To him with questions and with urine,
They for discov'ry flock, or curing.

*   *   *   *   *   *

He had been long t'wards mathematics,
Opticks, philosophy, and staticks,
Magick, horoscopy, astrology,
And was old dog at physiology :
But, as a dog that turns the spit,
Bestirs himself, and plies his feet
To climb the wheel, but all in vain,
His own weight brings him down again ;
And still he's in the self-same place,
Where at his setting out he was :

So, in the circle of the arts,
Did he advance his nat'ral parts:
Till falling back still, for retreat,
He fell to juggle, cant, and cheat:
For as those fowls that live in water
Are never wet, he did but smatter:
Whate'er he labour'd to appear,
His understanding still was clear,
Yet none a deeper knowledge boasted,
Since old Hodge Bacon, and Bob Grosted,
    *   *   *   *   *   *

Do not our great *Reformers* use
This SIDROPHEL to forebode news?
To write of victories next year,
And castles taken yet i'th' air?
Of battles fought at sea, and ships
Sunk, two years hence, the last eclipse?
A total o'erthrow giv'n the KING
In Cornwall, horse and foot, next spring?
And has not he point-blank foretold
Whatso'er the *Close Committee* would?
Made Mars and Saturn for the *cause*,
The Moon for *fundamental laws*;

The Ram, the Bull, the Goat, declare
Against the *Book of Common Prayer;*
The Scorpion take the *Protestation,*
And Bear engage for Reformation;
Made all the *royal stars* recant,
Compound, and take the covenant."

THE END.

MAURICE, PRINTER, FENCHURCH STREET.

Printed in the United States
219961BV00001B/223/A